Doing More Than Survive

A Gift for a Loved One in Jail or Prison

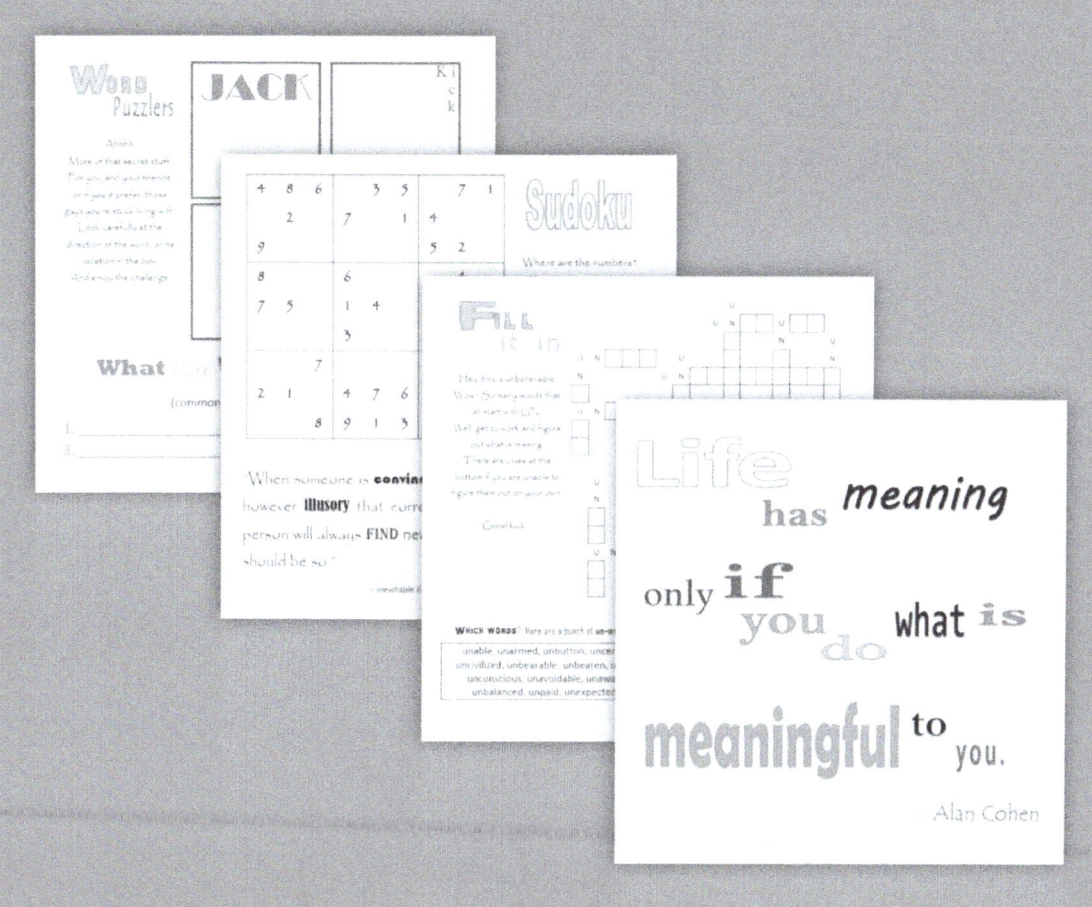

by C. Mahoney

Life is about choices...

It's **NOT** enough to just "survive" life and its **frustrations** and **annoyances**. You want to **EXCEL** in life, succeed, do well, **beat** the snot out of those who dare say that you can't get what you want and do what you want in life. Well, get up and do something about it. Do **MORE** than **JUST** survive.

You're in jail. Prison. And life **sucks**, sure. That's just the way it is right now. You're surrounded by morons. You're told what to do every day: get up, go to bed, get out of the restroom, eat, stop eating, walk here, don't walk here, go outside so we can take your stuff, stop, go, put your hands behind your back. It sucks! But what are you going to **DO** about it? Whine? Complain? Gripe to the nimrod bunked nearby? That won't do you any *good*.

Even though you're stuck there, **DO** something about it now. **Improve** yourself. **Read** at least one book every week. **WRITE** a letter to someone and tell them about your life there, your thoughts, your emotions, your goals, your plans, your hopes and dreams. **Work out**, every day, sculpting your body into something that you can be proud of, something strong and tough and durable. **Learn** a new language or teach someone yours. Make **choices** that are good for you, your mind, your body.

Do **MORE** than **JUST** survive each day there. **Improve** yourself.

Now turn the page and see what follows. You just might find a few things to help you along your way.

Challenge ONE

Unscramble these words

The LORD is my _____ and my _____.

    Whom shall I fear?

The LORD is the _____ of my life;

    Of whom shall I be afraid?

avtinslao

ttrhsneg   ihgtl

Psalm 27:1

Think about the words above and what they mean. Fear? Afraid? Life? What do they mean to you? Your life? Is it more about what you <u>do</u> or what you <u>think</u>? How does what you do flow from what you think? Thinking...doing. How are they related? Does one cause the other? Which comes first? Good questions that you should think about today as you breathe and smile and move about.

TRUST

Who do you TRUST the most?

- My mother/father
- My wife/husband
- My brother/sister
- My friend
- No one

What are you AFRAID of?

1. Getting shanked or stabbed?
2. Getting tazed or shot?
3. HIV?
4. Getting robbed?
5. Your dreams?
6. Getting a new charge?
7. Being deserted by your family?
8. Being lied to by those you trust?
9. Judgment Day?

Go ahead. Be honest. Think about your life, now, the things that surround you, and tell it like it is. You can't lie to yourself, you know. You might have your family fooled, and those knuckleheads you're housed with, but you won't fool that little arguer inside of your head that sees what you do and knows what you think. You.

Sudoku

3	1	6	9	7	5	4	2	8
8	2	5	4	6	1	3	9	7
4	7	9	8	2	3	1	6	5
1	6	8	2	3	7	5	4	9
7	4	3	1	5	9	6	8	2
5	9	2	6	8	4	7	3	1
2	8	4	7	1	6	9	5	3
6	3	1	5	9	2	8	7	4
9	5	7	3	4	8	2	1	6

Yay! It's time for fun, that 1-2-3-4-5-6-7-8-9 game of Where does it go? and What goes here? and Ahhhhhh!

Enjoy yourself and don't let the numbers get you down.

What are many people most **AFRAID** of?

1. *Public speaking* (yes, the #1 fear globally, talking in front of others…
2. *Spiders*, not bees or scorpions, but these critters…
3. *Flying*, and yet flying is statistically WAY safer than driving…
4. *Death*, Death is NOT the #1 fear…

Word Search

Hey, something is MISSing. What?
Well, words that start with the letters MIS-
They can be **horizontal**, **vertical**, **diagonal**, **forwards**, or **backwards**.
Can you find them?
I hope so.
Good luck, and don't make too many mistakes...

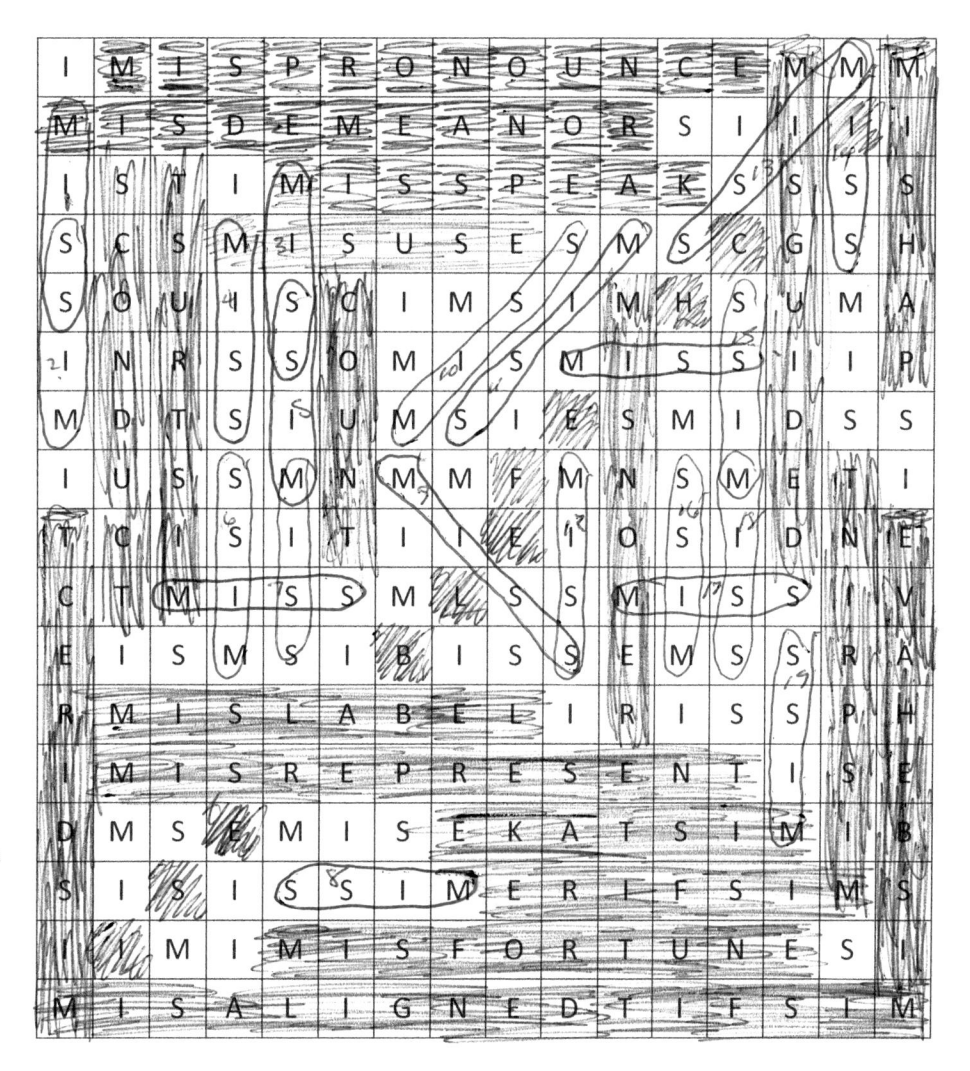

I	M	I	S	P	R	O	N	O	U	N	C	E	M	M	M		
M	I	S	D	E	M	E	A	N	O	R	S	I	I	I			
I	S	T	M	I	S	S	P	E	A	K	S	S	S	S			
S	C	S	M	I	S	U	S	E	S	M	S	C	G	S	H		
S	O	U	S	C	I	M	S	I	M	H	S	U	M	A			
I	N	R	S	O	M	I	S	M	I	S	S	I	P				
M	D	T	S	U	M	S	I	E	S	M	I	D	S	S			
I	U	S	S	M	N	M	M	F	M	N	S	M	E	T	I		
T	C	I	S	I	T	I	E	O	S	I	D	N	E				
C	T	M	I	S	S	M	L	S	S	M	I	S	S	V			
E	I	S	M	S	I	B	I	S	S	E	M	S	S	R	A		
R	M	I	S	L	A	B	E	L	I	R	I	S	S	P	H		
I	M	I	S	R	E	P	R	E	S	E	N	T	I	S	E		
D	M	S	E	M	I	S	E	K	A	T	S	I	M	I	B		
S	I	S	I	S	S	I	M	E	R	I	F	S	I	M	S		
I	I	M	I	M	I	S	F	O	R T	U	N	E	S	I			
M	I	S	A	L	I	G	N	E	D	T	I	F	S	I	M		

Find these words: ~~misaligned~~, ~~misbehave~~, ~~mischief~~, ~~misconduct~~, ~~miscount~~, ~~misdemeanor~~, ~~misdirect~~, ~~miserable~~, ~~misfire~~, ~~misfit~~, ~~misfortune~~, ~~misguided~~, ~~mishap~~, ~~mislabel~~, ~~misnomer~~, ~~misprint~~, ~~mispronounce~~, ~~misrepresent~~, ~~misspeak~~, ~~mistake~~, ~~mistrust~~, ~~misuse~~

Bonus: Can you find the four-letter word MISS? It's there, many times. How many can you find?

How many rectangles can YOU find?

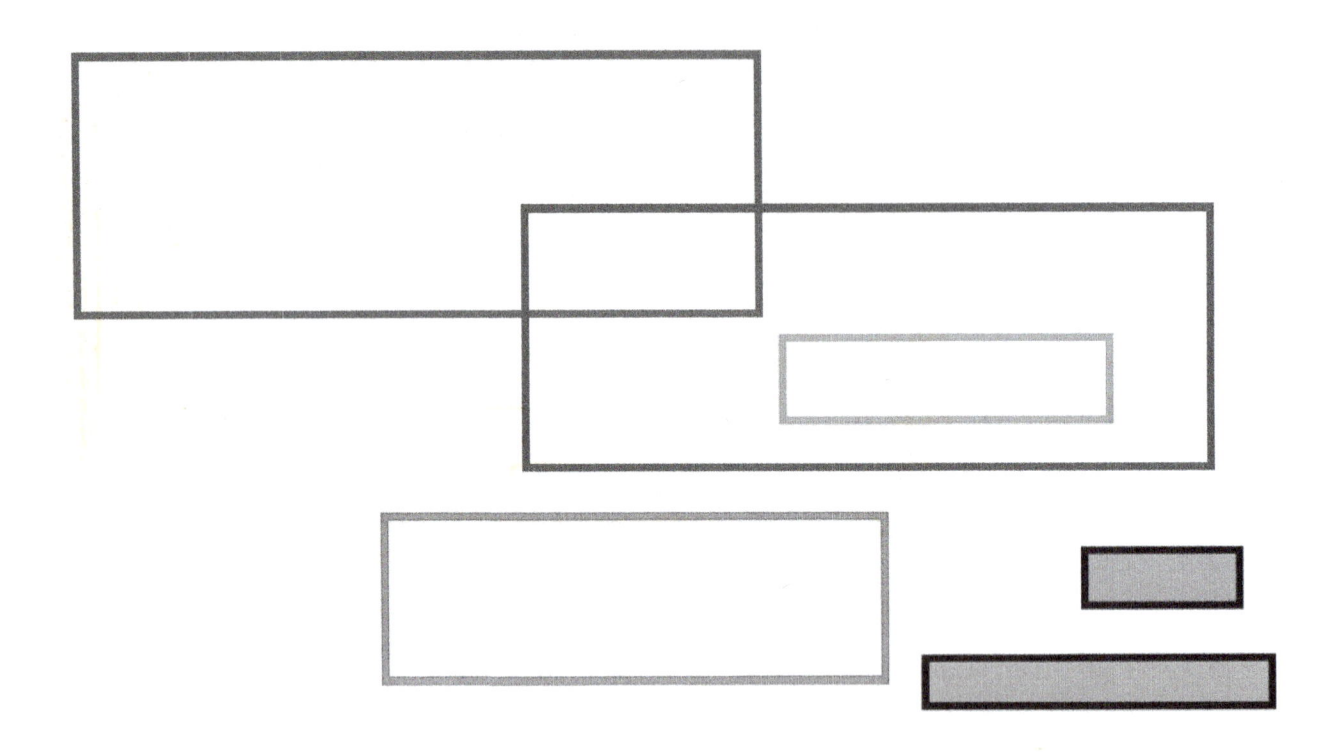

The answer is **NOT** six. Sorry. Try looking beyond the most **obvious**. Look for **overlapping** rectangles. That's right, rectangles that are placed on **TOP** of another.

Ten *action* **words** that describe ME

Think about what you **do**, what people see you **doing** with your *body*, your *mouth*, your *face*, your *hands*, your *feet*. Action is what you do (not what you say).

1		6	
2		7	
3		8	
4		9	
5		10	

Who am I?

_____
_____
_____
_____
_____

As I walked along a trail today, I came upon a worker busy at her tasks, and I reflected on my life and the things I do each day, and how insignificant they really are when you look at the big picture. Why get angry and scream and curse? Why hit and punch and hurt? I overstate my own importance so often, focused too strongly on MY desires and wants, me, me me, as if I alone were the only one that felt and thought and lived, ignoring what is around me. Today, I plan to be less self-absorbed.

The greatest danger for most of us is not that our aim is too high, but that it is too low and we reach it.

– Michelangelo

What are my goals?

My goals for today are…	My goals for tomorrow are…

My goals for next year are…	My goals for ten years from now are…

Answers

3	1	6	9	7	5	4	2	8
8	2	5	4	6	1	3	9	7
4	7	9	8	2	3	1	6	5
1	6	8	2	3	7	5	4	9
7	4	3	1	5	9	6	8	2
5	9	2	6	8	4	7	3	1
2	8	4	7	1	6	9	5	3
6	3	1	5	9	2	8	7	4
9	5	7	3	4	8	2	1	6

Scrambled Words: light, salvation, strength

Rectangles: 7

What do these words mean to you? Think for a moment. Then write a sentence or two.

Light:

Salvation:

Strength:

Challenge TWO

Unscramble these words

mrrtpaeoy
tsal
reovfer

Your circumstances are _____,

But your character will _____ _____.

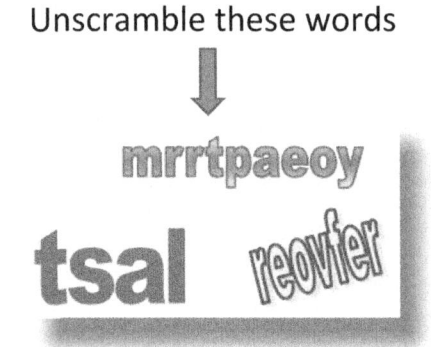

- by Rick Warren

Think about the words above and what they mean. Circumstances? Character? Both start with the same letter, C, but they are so different in quality and duration. Your circumstances surround you, while your character IS you. Your circumstances are almost impossible to control, yet your character is something that YOU develop and mold and create based on how you react to your circumstances. Your circumstances are temporary, but your character will last a lifetime. Don't let your circumstances dictate who you become.

Did you know: **agoraphobia** is the fear of open or public places

Steps. They are there because I need them to get from where I was to where I want to be. Sure, I could bypass them and make my own route through the pokey bushes and sticky plants and sharp cacti, but why put myself through that pain? These steps were put here to make my journey easier, so I would know where I was headed and how to get there. I just need to put one foot in front of the other. Step, step, step.

What would **you write** here IF you could?
Psst! **YOu** can!

Pick One

Circle it, write it, explain your choice. You can only pick one. No cheating! This activity gets you thinking outside the box, and maybe, outside of your cell.

1	Which is **prettier**, a baby daughter or the smile on the face of a man upon release?
2	Which is **stronger**, a pile of dog doo or a man who can do 1,000 pushups?
3	Which is **smarter**, a word spoken in kindness or a punch in the face?
4	Which is **cleaner**, a man after he has showered or the mind of an innocent man?
5	Which is **straighter**, the gate that holds you in or a taxi driving you home?
6	Which is **uglier**, an enraged convict or a condescending guard?
7	Which is **colder**, an irritated wife or a courtroom prosecutor?

Word Search

Hey, it's that time to find more words.
They can be **horizontal**, **vertical**, **diagonal**, **forwards**, or **backwards**.
What do these words have in common?
Why are they here?
What do they mean?
Stop asking questions and get to searching, now.
The clock is ticking.

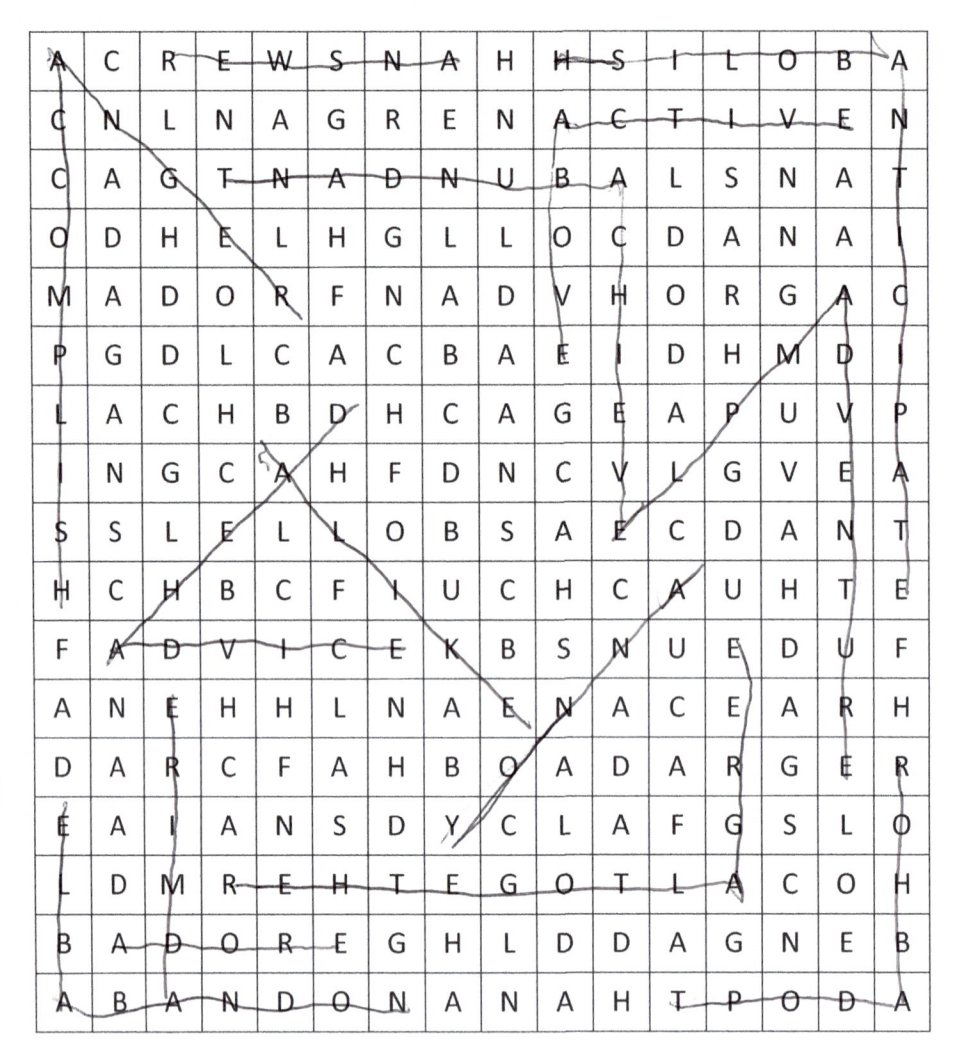

A	C	R	E	W	S	N	A	H	H	S	I	L	O	B	A
C	N	L	N	A	G	R	E	N	A	C	T	I	V	E	N
C	A	G	T	N	A	D	N	U	B	A	L	S	N	A	T
O	D	H	E	L	H	G	L	L	O	C	D	A	N	A	I
M	A	D	O	R	F	N	A	D	V	H	O	R	G	A	C
P	G	D	L	C	A	C	B	A	E	I	D	H	M	D	I
L	A	C	H	B	D	H	C	A	G	E	A	P	U	V	P
I	N	G	C	A	H	F	D	N	C	V	L	G	V	E	A
S	S	L	E	L	L	O	B	S	A	E	C	D	A	N	T
H	C	H	B	C	F	I	U	C	H	C	A	U	H	T	E
F	A	D	V	I	C	E	K	B	S	N	U	E	D	U	F
A	N	E	H	H	L	N	A	E	N	A	C	E	A	R	H
D	A	R	C	F	A	H	B	O	A	D	A	R	G	E	R
E	A	I	A	N	S	D	Y	C	L	A	F	G	S	L	O
L	D	M	R	E	H	T	E	G	O	T	L	A	C	O	H
B	A	D	O	R	E	G	H	L	D	D	A	G	N	E	B
A	B	A	N	D	O	N	A	N	A	H	T	P	O	D	A

Find these words: ~~abandon~~, ~~abhor~~, ~~able~~, ~~abolish~~, ~~above~~, abundant, ~~accomplish~~, ~~achieve~~, ~~active~~, ~~adopt~~, ~~admire~~, ~~adore~~, adventure, ~~advise~~, ~~agree~~, ~~ahead~~, ~~alike~~, all, ~~altogether~~, ~~ample~~, ~~anger~~, ~~annoy~~, answer, ~~anticipate~~

Word Puzzlers

Ahhhh! It's time for us to explore the world of secret words, confusing to those who can't see beyond the letters and numbers and symbols. But you? You're smart. So this will be a snap. Easy. Simple. Enjoy the challenge. See if anyone else can solve them...

NRG	GR8
sweet10	→ thehill

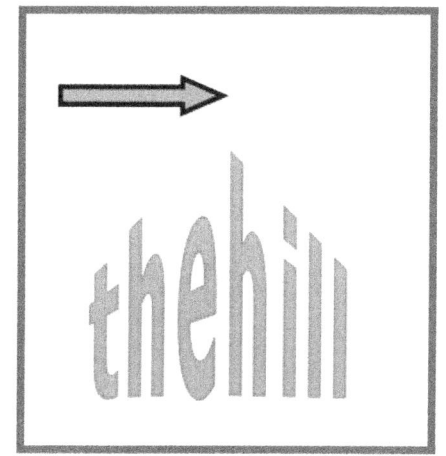

What four words do you see?

(common words or phrases we say)

1. _____
2. _____
3. _____
4. _____

How many rectangles can you find?

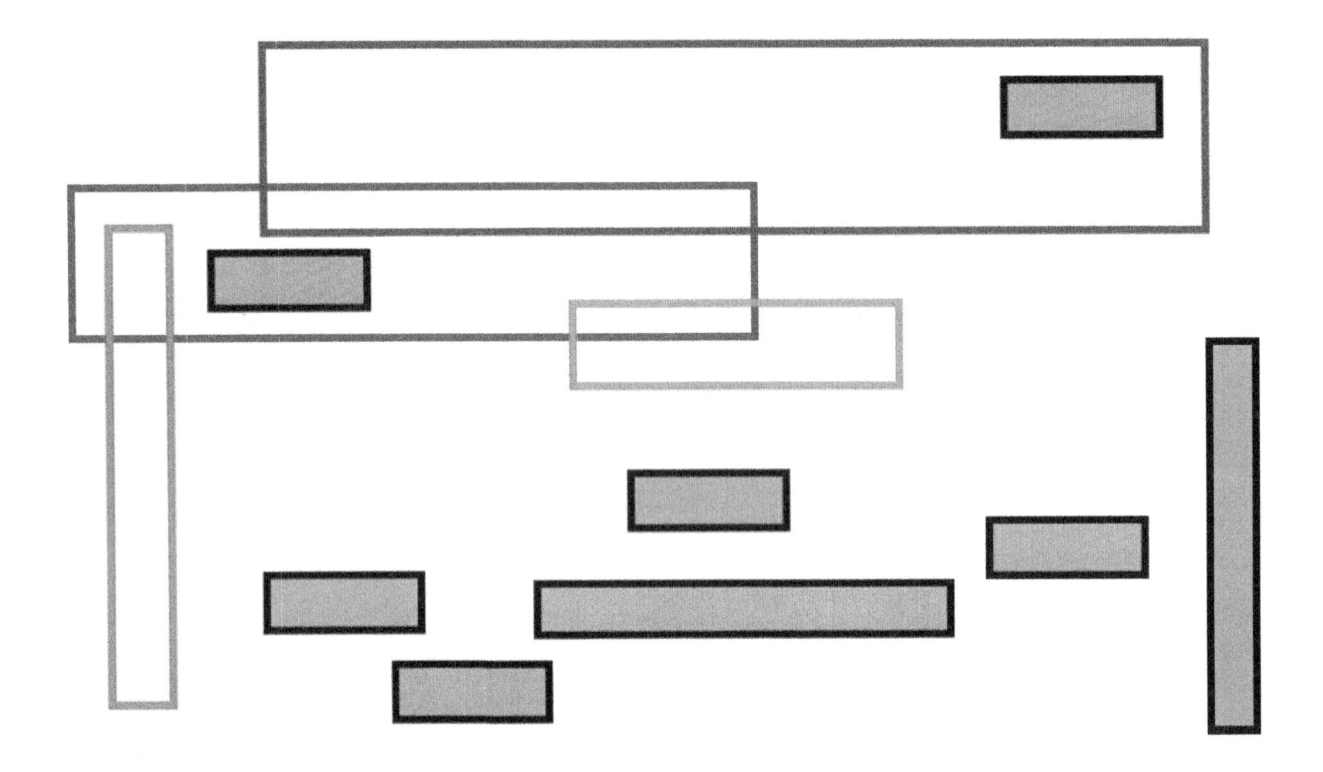

There are **three** types of rectangles here. One: those that are **shaded**, easy to see. Two: those that are clear, not shaded, **transparent**. Three: the **overlapped** triangles that are formed when two rectangles, well, you know…overlap.

Sudoku

2	8	5	6	4	1	9	7	3
4	3	1	5	9	7	6	8	2
6	9	7	2	3	8	1	4	5
7	1	2	3	6	5	8	9	4
3	4	8	1	7	9	5	2	6
9	5	6	8	2	4	3	1	7
8	2	9	7	5	6	4	3	1
1	6	3	4	8	2	7	5	9
5	7	4	9	1	3	2	6	8

Something is missing. Numbers. 1-2-3-4-5-6-7-8-9 should be on every vertical **column** and on every horizontal **row** and in every 3x3 **square**. So find them. They're in your mind, along with a lot of other useless stuff.

Four **things** my **mother** taught ME...

1 *to always* _____
2 *to always* _____
3 *to always* _____
4 *to always* _____

There is no security in this life. There is only opportunity.

- Douglas MacArthur

Answers

2	8	5	6	4	1	9	7	3
4	3	1	5	9	7	6	8	2
6	9	7	2	3	8	1	4	5
7	1	2	3	6	5	8	9	4
3	4	8	1	7	9	5	2	6
9	5	6	8	2	4	3	1	7
8	2	9	7	5	6	4	3	1
1	6	3	4	8	2	7	5	9
5	7	4	9	1	3	2	6	8

Scrambled Words: temporary, last, forever

Word Puzzlers: energy, great, sweeten, over the hill

Rectangles: 16

Why am I here?

I am on Earth to _____
_____

I am in this room to _____
_____

Use the word "to" and action words (not "because" and a reason). Are you here to fight and argue and steal and hurt others? No! You are not. Think about why you are really here, alive, today, blessed with the ability to move about and think and speak. Think. Write. Then share with others…

Challenge THREE

Unscramble these words ↓

> Consider the work of God,
> For who can make _____
> what he has made _____?
>
> - Ecclesiastes 7:13

gsaitrht
ecokrod

Think about the two scrambled words above and what they mean. They are opposites. Who can...? Can you? Some things just are, like now, where you are, your neighbors, your restrictions. Can you walk out of this room and go where you want? No. Are you free? No. You can't change that, so consider why you are here and what you can change.

Change

What can you change?

- Your attitude?
- Your knowledge?
- Your beliefs?
- Your emotions?

What do you know?

Can you tell me what these **acronyms** stand for? An acronym is a word (like radar) or an abbreviation (like FBI) that is spelled from the first letters of a phrase. Do you know these?

AIDS = acquired _____ syndrome
Radar = radio _____ and _____
NAACP = National _____ for the Advancement of _____ _____
NATO = _____ Atlantic _____ Organization
AM = _____ modulation (radio waves); or ante _____ (time)
FM = _____ modulation (radio waves)
PM = post _____ (time)
HIV = human _____ virus
FBI = Federal _____ of _____
CIA = Central intelligence Agency
p.s. = post _____
DC = District of Columbia
OJ = _____ juice
GTA = _____ theft _____
GBI = _____ bodily _____
L-WOP = life-without the _____

Did you know: **claustrophobia** is the fear of closed or narrow spaces

WORD Puzzlers

Ahhhh!
More of that secret stuff.
For you, and your friends,
or if you'd prefer, those
guys you're stuck living with.
Look carefully at the
direction of the word, or its
location in the box.
And enjoy the challenge.

| JACK | Kick (top right corner) |
| H I L L (bottom to top) | PAYMENT (vertical) |

What four words do you see?

(common words or phrases we say)

1. _____
2. _____
3. _____
4. _____

I passed a leaf and had to stop, curious about what was within and wondering how to bring out its inner beauty, the parts that make it alive and healthy. Just like me. How do I get people to see the real me, the me that lives within and desires peace and comfort and happiness? Sometimes that ugly guy emerges, with shouts and selfishness and rudeness, but I want the other guy to be seen and heard. It's up to me who they see, my choice, my decision.

Sudoku

4	8	6	2	3	5	9	7	1
3	2	5	7	9	1	4	8	6
9	7	1	8	6	4	5	2	3
8	3	9	6	5	2	1	4	7
7	5	2	1	4	9	6	3	8
1	6	4	3	8	7	2	5	9
6	9	7	5	2	8	3	1	4
2	1	3	4	7	6	8	9	5
5	4	8	9	1	3	7	6	2

Where are the numbers?
They are in your mind.
That's right.

Now go sort through those filing cabinets and find the 1-2-3-4-5-6-7-8-9.
They might be hiding.
Peek-a-boo, I see you.

"When someone is **convinced** of a positive **correlation**, however **illusory** that correlation can be shown to be, that person will always **FIND** new confirmations and **justify** why it should be so."

- Inevitable Illusions: How Mistakes of Reason Rule our Minds, page 122

Pick One

Circle it, write it, explain your choice. You can only pick one. No cheating! This activity gets you thinking outside the box, and maybe, outside the cell.

1 Which is **smoother**, an inmate telling a story or warmed-up peanut butter?

2 Which is **flatter**, the lie you just heard from your bunkie or a piece of old newspaper?

3 Which is **faster**, the word F—K blurted at another man or a silent prayer pushed toward heaven?

4 Which is **scarier**, sitting in a courtroom chair or kicking off your shoes to fight?

5 Which is **taller**, a queen attacking your opponent's king or a letter from your brother?

6 Which is **warmer**, the girl who visits you or an extra blanket in the winter?

7 Which is **easier** to understand, the remote control or your Out Date?

Fill it in

Hey, this is unbelievable. Wow! So many words that all start with UN- Well, get to work and figure out what is missing. There are clues at the bottom if you are unable to figure them out on your own.

Good luck...

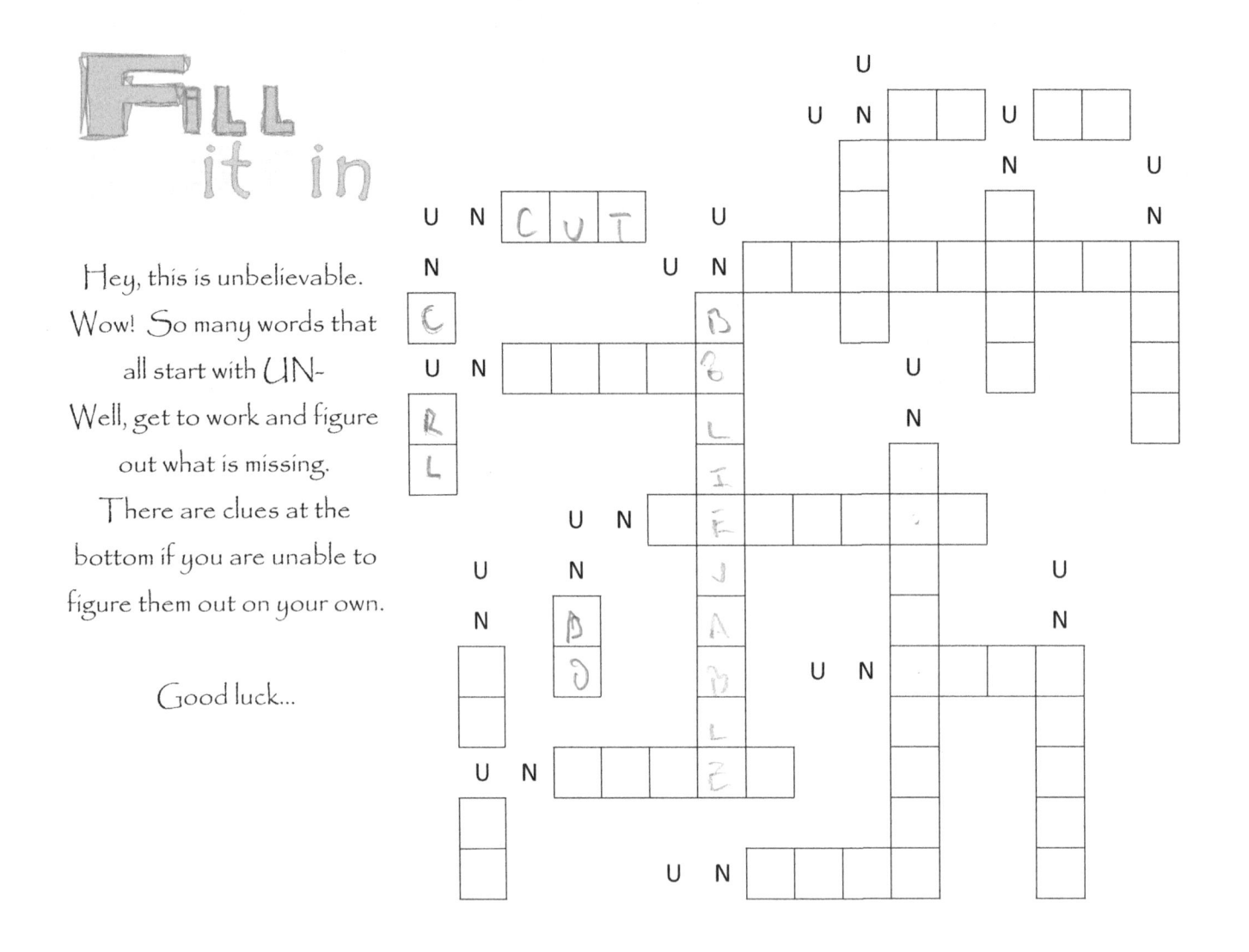

Which words? Here are a bunch of **un-words**. You need <u>sixteen</u> of them. The rest are here to annoy you.

unable, unarmed, unbutton, uncertain, uncurl, unearth, unfair, undo, uncirculated, uncivilized, unbearable, unbeaten, uneasy, unemployed, unload, uncut, unconcerned, unconscious, unavoidable, unaware, uncover, uneven, unclean, undress, unstop, unbalanced, unpaid, unexpected, uncommon, unbelievable, unusual, unequal,

Life is a daring adventure or it is nothing at all.

— Helen Keller

How many rectangles can YOU find?

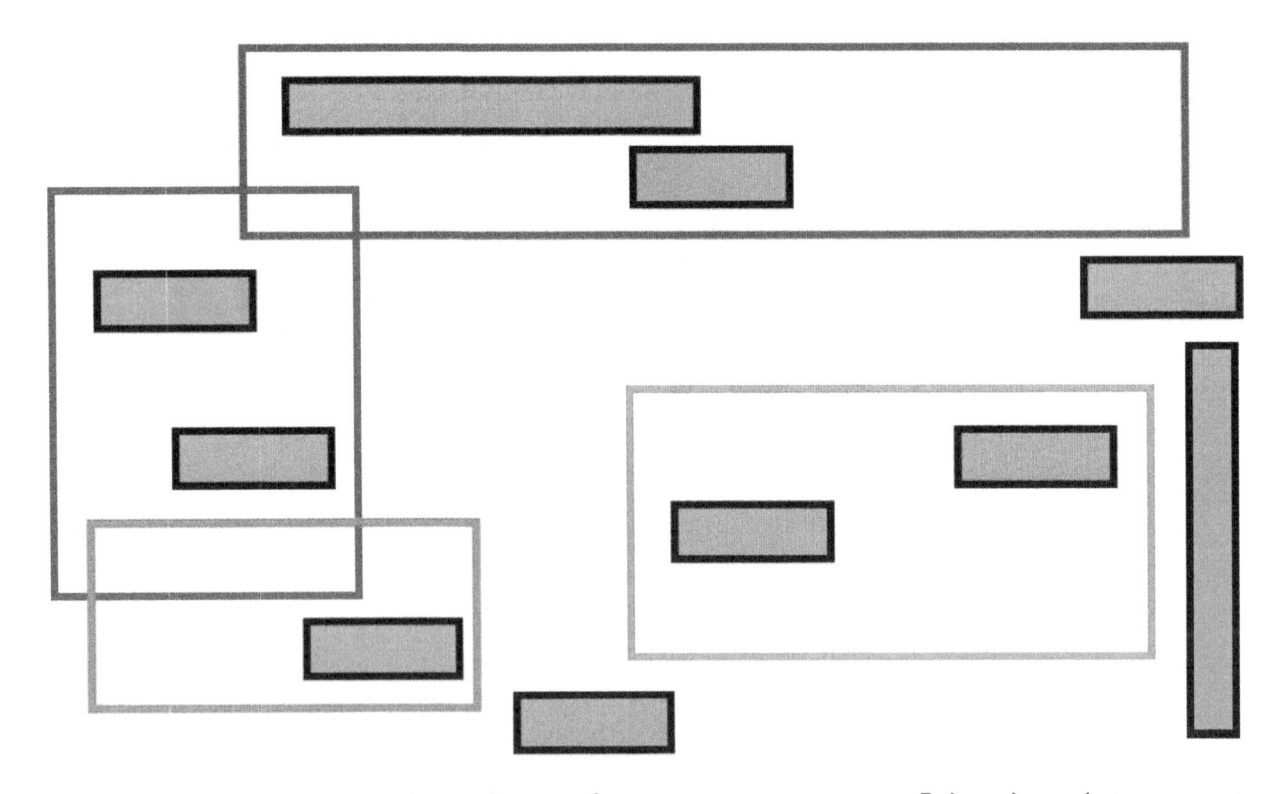

Rectangles, more **rectangles**, and more RECTANGLES. Did you know that a square is a rectangle? It is. A triangle, on the other hand, is NOT a rectangle. Everyone knows that, you, me, and that knucklehead who sleeps in the bunk nearby. Well, maybe he doesn't know it. He's not that bright.

Answers

AIDS	acquired immunodeficiency syndrome
Radar	radio detecting and ranging
NAACP	National Association for the Advancement of Colored Peoples
NATO	North Atlantic Treaty Organization
AM	amplitude modulation; or ante meridiem (time)
FM	frequency modulation
PM	post meridiem
HIV	human immunodeficiency virus
FBI	Federal Bureau of Investigation
CIA	Central Intelligence Agency
p.s.	post script
DC	District of Columbia
OJ	orange juice
GTA	grand theft auto
GBI	great bodily injury
L-WOP	life-without the possibility of parole

4	8	6	2	3	5	9	7	1
3	2	5	7	9	1	4	8	6
9	7	1	8	6	4	5	2	3
8	3	9	6	5	2	1	4	7
7	5	2	1	4	9	6	3	8
1	6	4	3	8	7	2	5	9
6	9	7	5	2	8	3	1	4
2	1	3	4	7	6	8	9	5
5	4	8	9	1	3	7	6	2

Word Puzzlers: hijack, corner kick, uphill, down payment

Scrambled Words: straight, crooked

Un- Words: unavoidable, unaware, unbelievable, uncertain, uncivilized, uncover, uncurl, uneasy, unequal, unfair, undo, unload, unpaid, undress, unstop, unusual

Rectangles: 16

It **is** NEVER too **late** to **learn.**

Challenge FOUR

__n G__d I h__v__ p__t m__ tr__st;
__ w__ll n__t b__ __fr____d.
Wh__t c__n m__n d__ t__ m__?

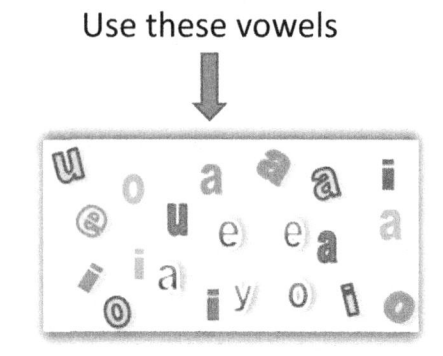

Use these vowels

Psalm 56:11

Think about the words above and what they mean. What is the worst that a man can do to you?

...to your body

...to your emotions

...to your mind

Sudoku

8	7	6	4	9	2	5	1	3
3	4	9	8	1	5	2	7	6
2	5	1	7	3	6	9	4	8
5	8	7	3	6	1	4	9	2
4	1	3	2	7	9	6	8	5
9	6	2	5	4	8	1	3	7
1	2	8	9	5	7	3	6	4
7	9	4	6	2	3	8	5	1
6	3	5	1	8	4	7	2	9

Again, let's try the digit game.
One, two, three.
Where do they go?
Find out...

Enjoy yourself.

What do YOU laugh at?

1. I laugh at _____
2. I laugh at _____
3. I laugh at _____
4. I laugh at _____

Did you know: **acrophobia** is the fear of high places

A leaf shows just what it is, not what it wants to be. The spots and cracks, the withered frailty and age, the crackling skin and water damage. It's all there, seen by any who pass by, just like the real you, the guy who jokes at others, words tossed out to lift you higher and bring them down to where you don't want to be. Guys see that, hear it. It's you. Don't fool yourself into thinking that they don't. You can't hide who you really are. Consider that when you open your mouth to speak.

WORD Puzzlers

Ahhhh!
More of that secret stuff.
For you, and your friends,
or if you'd prefer, those
guys you're stuck living with.
Look carefully at the
direction of the word, or its
location in the box.
And enjoy the challenge.

play play	WAYS
sit ───── your **bunk**	lotso**IAM**ftrouble

What four words do you see?
(common words or phrases we say)

1. _____ 2. _____
3. _____ 4. _____

Word Search

Hey, it's about time you admit the truth. **TRUTH!** It's here, on this page, over and over again. Can you find it? It can be **horizontal**, **vertical**, **diagonal**, **forwards**, or **backwards**.

One, two, lots and lots...

Psalm 117:2 says, "The truth of the LORD endures forever."

What is this "truth" that the Psalmist is talking about?

_____
_____
_____
_____

How many rectangles can YOU find?

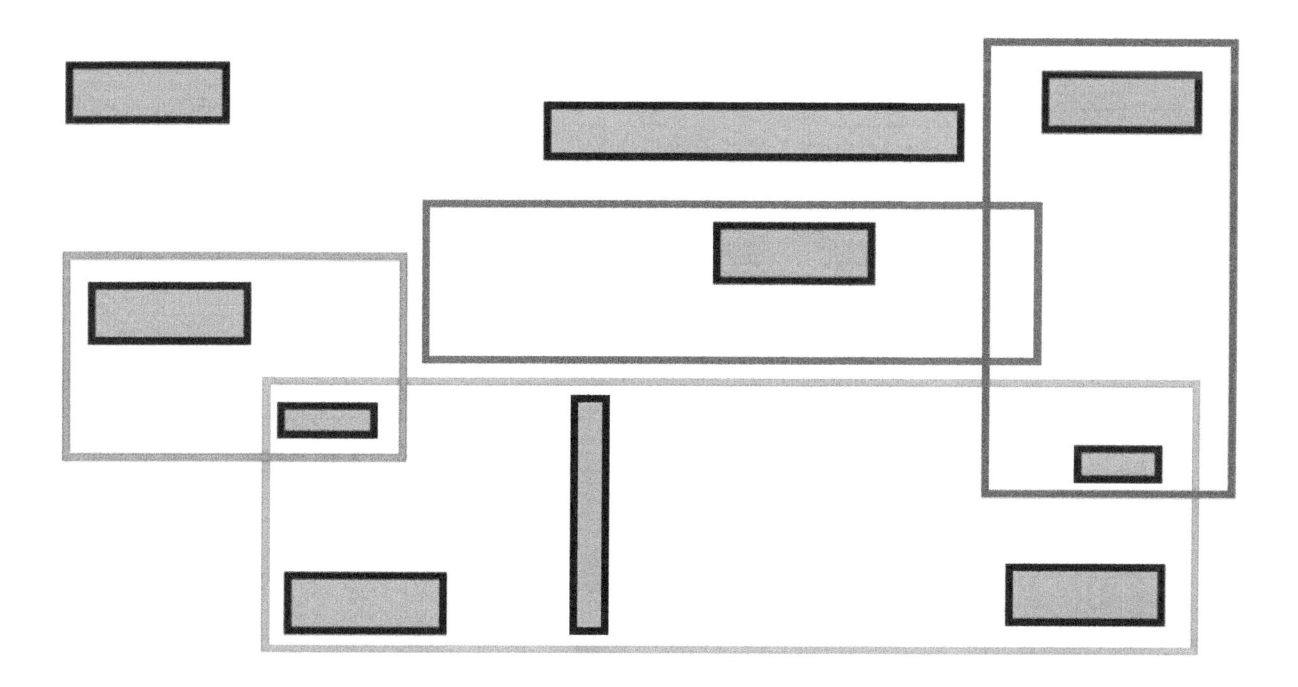

Rectangles and **squares** are part of a group called *quadrilaterals*. Quad- means four, of course, just as tri- means three, and bi- means two. Easy! In this group of four-sided polygons are a few more shapes: **trapezoids, parallelograms, rombii** (the plural of rhombus), and **irregular quadrilaterals**.

Grab a pencil and write SOMETHING positive about *yourself*!

Pick One

Circle it, write it, explain your choice. You can only pick one. No cheating! This activity gets you thinking outside the box, and maybe, outside the cell.

1 Which is **heavier**, the guilt you carry or the fat guy who sleeps all day?

2 Which is **nearer**, the day you are free or the moment you accept responsibility for your crime?

3 Which is **roomier**, the cell you live in or the opportunities that await you on the outside?

4 Who is more **miserable**, the guy who was innocent or the guy who has to listen to him every day?

5 Who is more **demanding**, the guy who just got there or the guy who has been there for too long?

6 Which is more **serious**, your case or the words your mother spoke to you about changing your ways?

7 Which produces more **yawns**, the night before your court date or a guy who is there on violation?

Life has meaning only if you do what is meaningful to you.

— Alan Cohen

Answers

8	7	6	4	9	2	5	1	3
3	4	9	8	1	5	2	7	6
2	5	1	7	3	6	9	4	8
5	8	2	3	6	1	4	9	7
4	1	3	2	7	9	6	8	5
9	6	7	5	4	8	1	3	2
1	2	8	9	5	7	3	6	4
7	9	4	6	2	3	8	5	1
6	3	5	1	8	4	7	2	9

Missing Letters: In God I have put my trust; I will not be afraid. What can man do to me? **Psalm 56:11**

Word Puzzlers: double-play, sideways, sit on your bunk, I am in lots of trouble

Rectangles: 17

Remember Psalm 56:11 when someone accosts you, verbally or physically. Don't sweat it. Let it go, like water off a duck's back. Just let it go...

What do these words mean to you?

put:

afraid:

do:

Challenge FIVE

Unscramble these words ⬇

Two are better than one,

because they have a good _reward_ for their labor.

For if they _fall_, one will lift up his companion.

But woe to him who is _alone_ when he falls,

for he has no one to _help_ him up.

owt   derarw
    enola
lafl   leph

Ecclesiastes 4:9-10

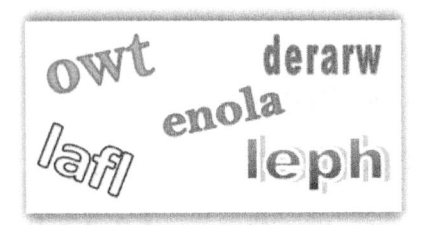

Think about the words above and what they mean. Labor? Alone? Help?

Alone

Is it good to be alone sometimes? When?

- Reading a book
- Writing a letter
- Playing cards
- Thinking
- Watching tv
- Praying
- Sleeping
- Walking

Word Search

Hey, it's that time again to find words.

They can be **horizontal**, **vertical**, **diagonal**, **forwards**, or **backwards**.

These words are words you might be familiar with. Just look around you now, that place you are forced to call "home."

One day it won't be...

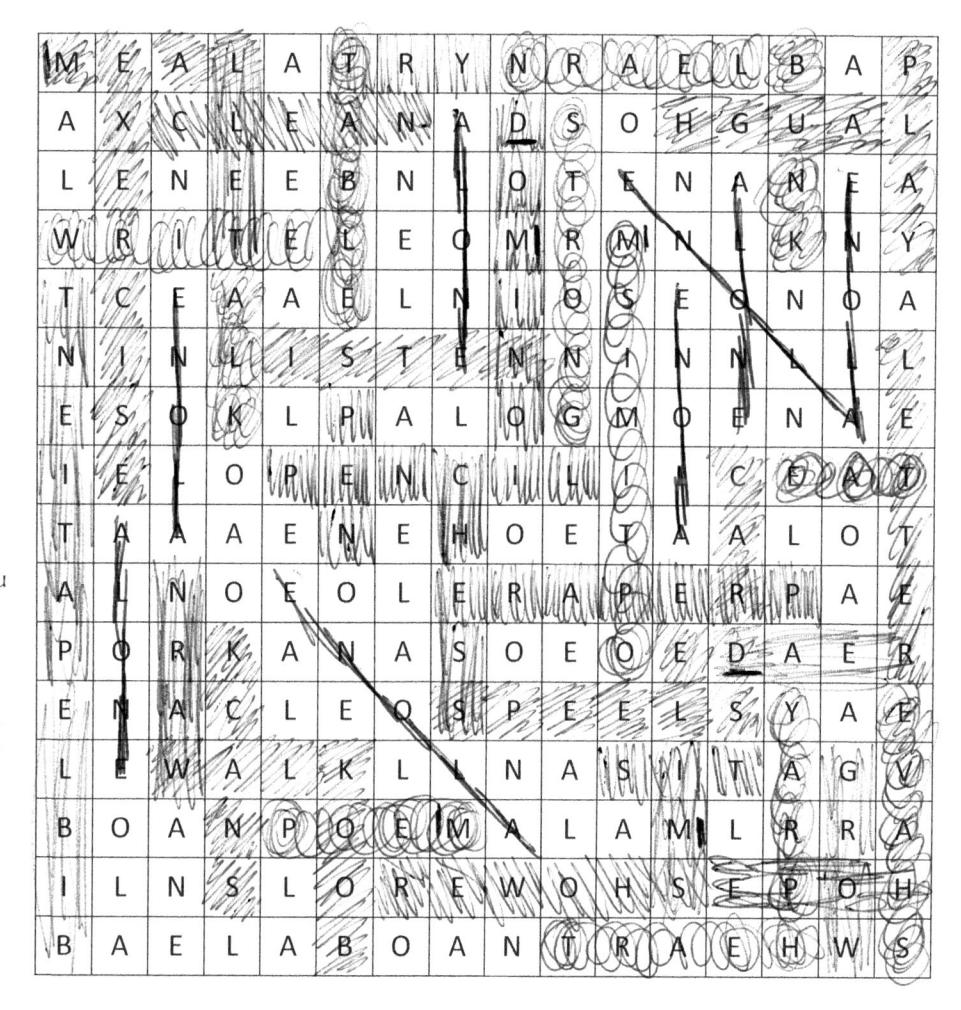

```
M E A L A T R Y N R A E L B A P
A X C L E A N A D S O H G U A L
L E N E E B N O T E N A N E A
W R I T E L E O M R M N L K N Y
T C E A A E L N I O S E O N O A
N I N L I S T E N N I N N L L
E S O K L P A L O G M O E N A E
I E L O P E N C I L I C E A T
T A A E N E H O E T A A L O T
A L N O E O L E R A P E R P A E
P O R K A N A S O E O E D A E R
E N A C L E O S P E E L S Y A E
L W A L K L I N A S I T A G V
B O A N P O E M A L A M L R R A
I L N S L O R E W O H S E P O H
B A E L A B O A N T R A E H W S
```

Find these words: write, letter, read, book, play, cards, sleep, talk, listen, smile, laugh, walk, exercise, eat, snack, meal, toll, warn, prepare, sit, domino, chess, pencil, pen, clean, shower, shave, bunk, table, poem, Bible, pray, hope, try, patient, learn, grow, strong, mind, heart, optimism

Bonus: How many times can you find the word ALONE in this Word Search?

Did you know: a **shyster** is an unscrupulous lawyer or politician

Sudoku

9	2	4	7	3	5	1	8	6
5	7	1	6	8	2	4	9	3
6	3	8	4	1	9	5	2	7
1	5	2	3	9	8	7	6	4
3	6	9	5	4	7	8	1	2
8	4	7	2	6	1	9	3	5
2	8	6	1	7	4	3	5	9
7	9	5	8	2	3	6	4	1
4	1	3	9	5	6	2	7	8

Numbers, again, missing because they wandered off in search of something greater.
Your job is to find them and put them back where they belong.
1-2-3-4-5-6-7-8-9,

Words I say, but shouldn't...

1 _____
2 _____
3 _____
4 _____

Word Puzzlers

Some are easy, some are hard, and some are not written like they are supposed to be.
Well, they are this way on purpose.
Figure out why and you'll solve the problem.

Enjoy!

overs	GROUND (reversed)
Ding	d r a i n (vertical)

What four words do you see?

(common words or phrases we say)

1. _____
2. _____
3. _____
4. _____

A squirrel crawls among the fallen leaves, looking for food. That's what it does all day long, looking and searching and hoping to find something tasty and filling. How about you? What do you search for all day? Someone to make fun of, laugh at? Someone to listen to your tales of woe and unfairness and innocence? Someone to be impressed with your sexual conquests and fights and drug-induced exploits? Pick wisely what you search for each day.

How many rectangles can YOU find?

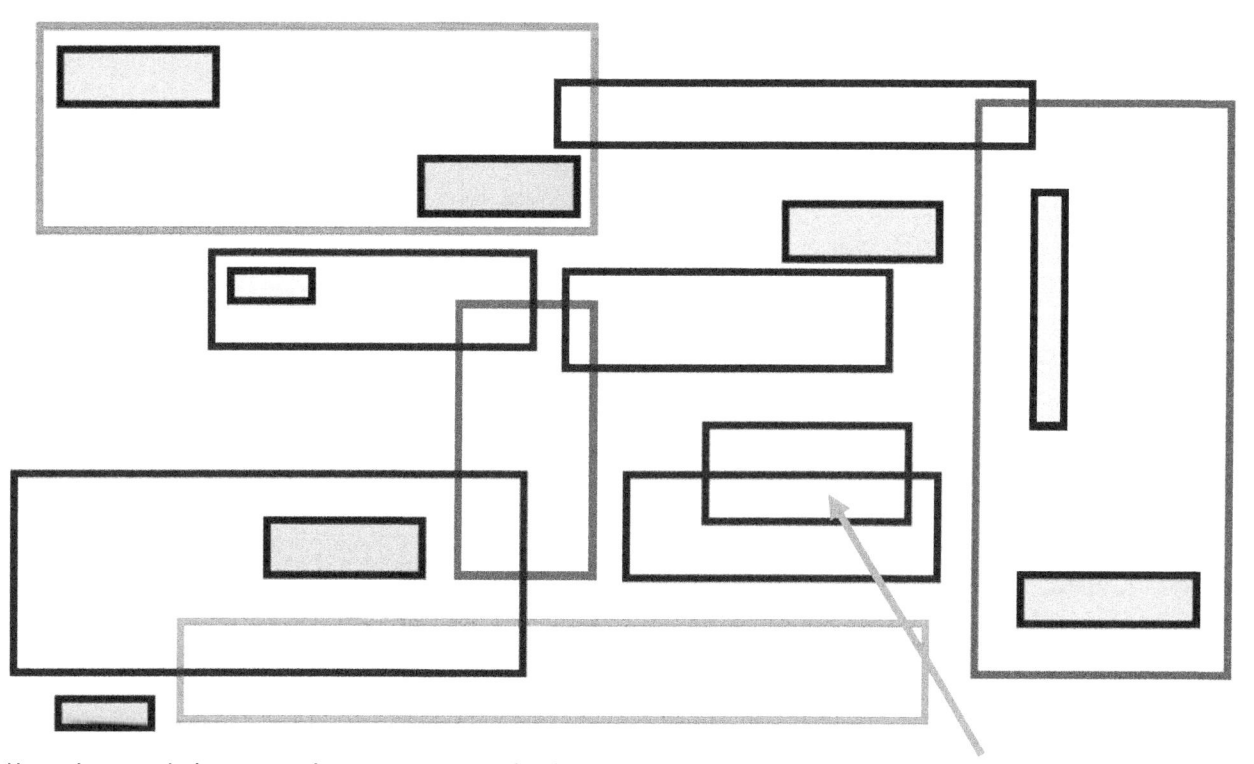

Now, this puzzle has something unique in it. Look carefully. Sometimes a rectangle has two smaller rectangles on the inside. This one does. Pay attention to this new idea or else you'll never figure out how many rectangles I've hidden in these designs. Now, what did they say about old dogs and new tricks?

The meaning of life is to give life meaning.

— Ken Hudgins

Why do you want to be free?

List eight things you want to do on your first day of freedom.

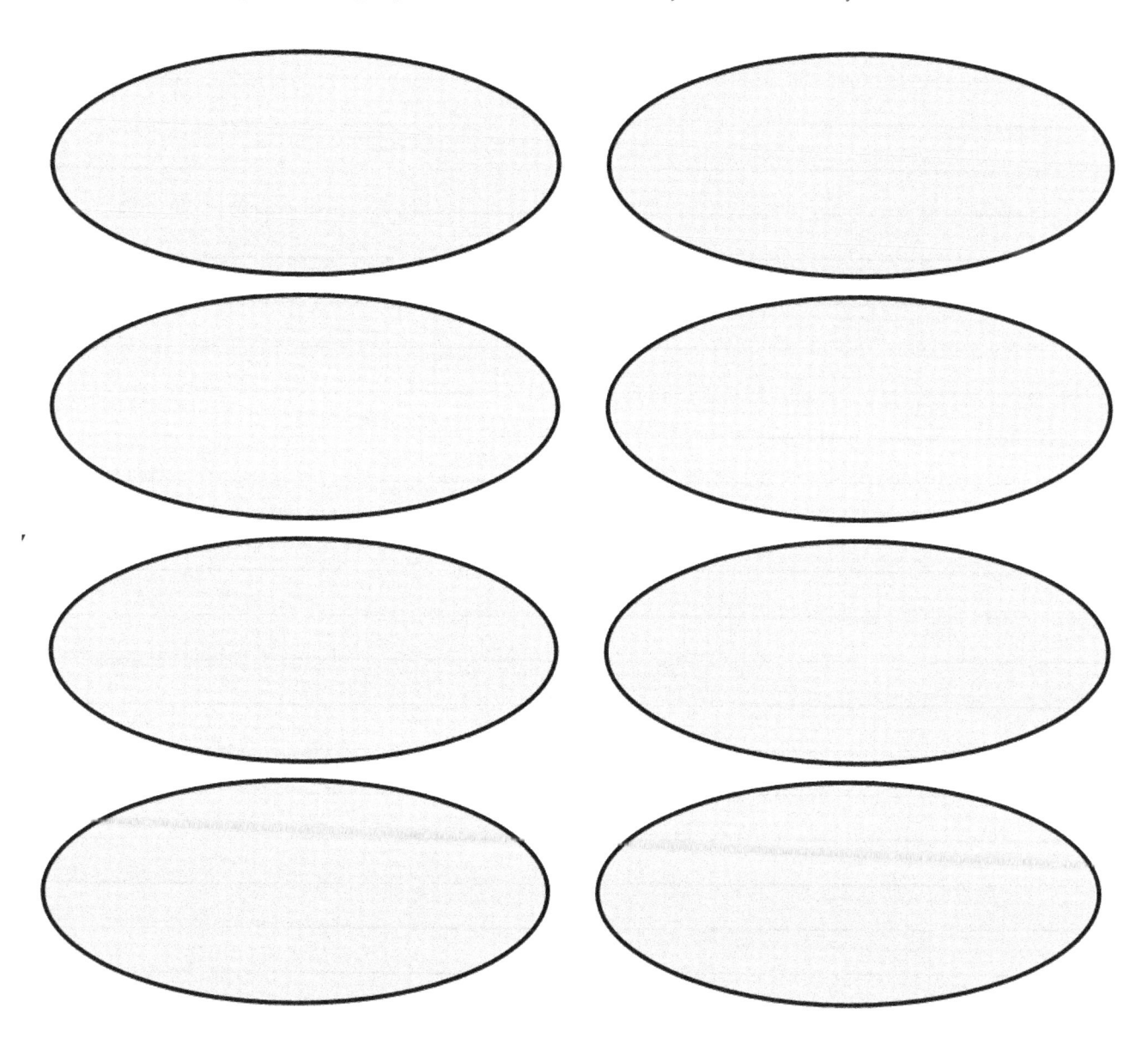

Answers

9	2	4	7	3	5	1	8	6
5	7	1	6	8	2	4	9	3
6	3	8	4	1	9	5	2	7
1	5	2	3	9	8	7	6	4
3	6	9	5	4	7	8	1	2
8	4	7	2	6	1	9	3	5
2	8	6	1	7	4	3	5	9
7	9	5	8	2	3	6	4	1
4	1	3	9	5	6	2	7	8

Scrambled Words: two, reward, fall, alone, help

Word Puzzlers: leftovers, background, loading, down the drain

Rectangles: 27

What is the difference between two and *alone*?

Challenge SIX

Unscramble these words

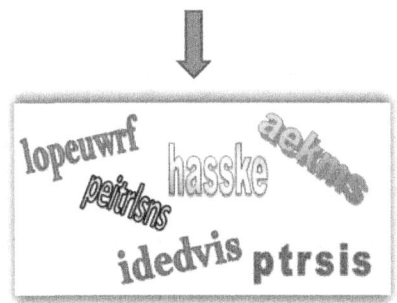

lopeuwrf   hasske   aekms
peirlsns
idedvis   ptrsis

The voice of the LORD...

...is _____

..._____ the cedars of Lebanon

..._____ the flames of fire

...makes the deer give _____

..._____ the forest bare

......_____ the wilderness

- **Psalm 29**

The voice within you that tells you to "Stop!" Is that you? or someone else?

Sudoku

2	3	5	6	7	9	1	4	8
7	4	9	8	1	5	6	3	2
1	8	6	3	4	2	5	7	9
4	1	3	9	2	7	8	5	6
5	6	8	1	3	4	2	9	7
9	7	2	5	8	6	4	1	3
8	5	4	2	9	3	7	6	1
6	9	1	7	5	8	3	2	4
3	2	7	4	6	1	9	8	5

Again, it's up to you to save the world by completing the 1-2-3-4-5-6-7-8-9 game of Nine. Use your super-sleuthing skills to determine what is missing from this puzzle. It's up to you!

What does the world need to be saved from?

1 from _____

2 from _____

3 from _____

Did you know: **zip code** stands for Zone Improvement Plan (ZIP)

An arch spans a trail Because it is interesting, hikers see it and stop, to look, to walk through, to take a photo and remember their trek. This is what awaits you, opportunities to see and feel and admire, trails made by others or new ones that you blaze yourself. Life. It's out there, waiting to be lived. You just gotta survive this time, these days. Be positive, be hopeful, and do your time. One day you'll be free. One day, and then you'll be the first to notice something different or unique.

Word Puzzlers

More, yes, of the puzzlers to get you to scratching your head and saying "What?" Try to look for words you know, words within words, or maybe how a number sounds, or where all the arrows are pointing...

Clues, prompts. Good luck...

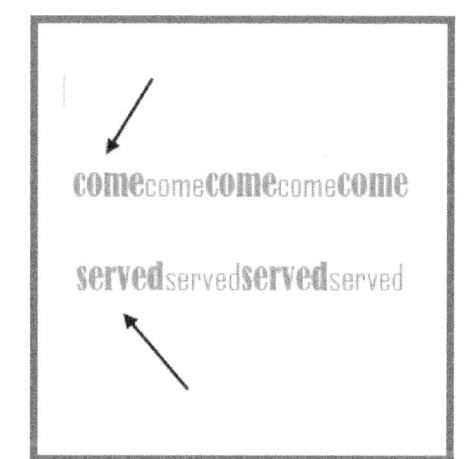

Box 1: come come COME come come / served served SERVED served (with arrows pointing down and up)

Box 2: mybo**feelIT**nes

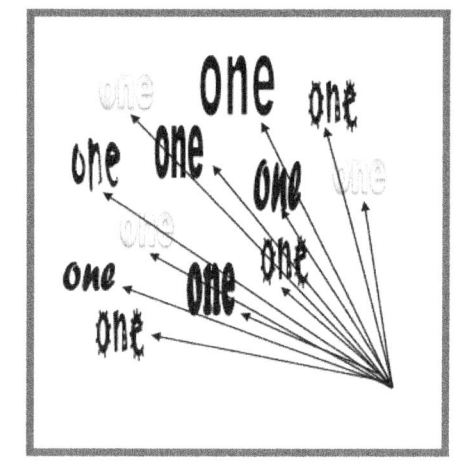

Box 3: one one ONE one one one one one one one one one one (with many arrows pointing to them)

Box 4: SUR**5**

What four words do you see?

(common words or phrases we say)

1. _____
2. _____
3. _____
4. _____

Word Search

Hey, every **single** word in this **double** puzzle is doubled, for your pleasure, a two-for-one special. See if you can find them before you start seeing double.

They can be horizontal, vertical, diagonal, forwards, or backwards.

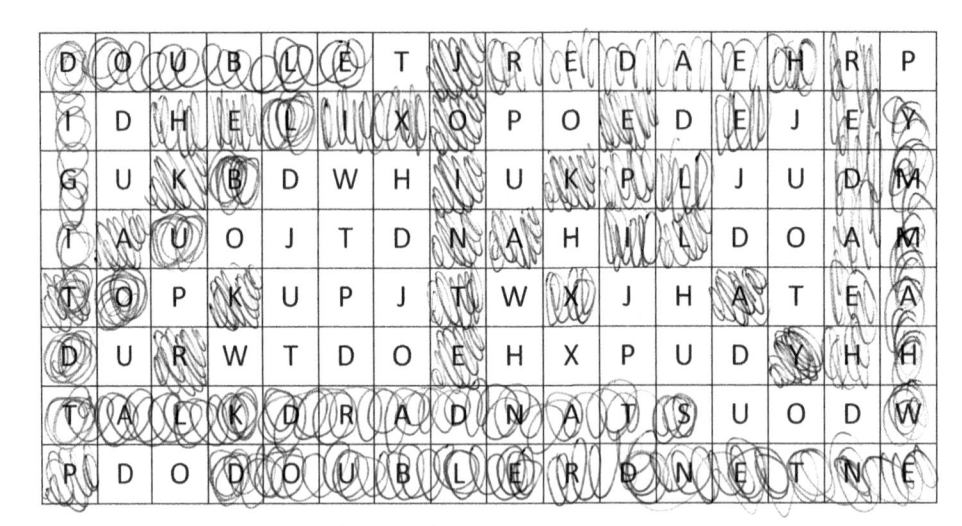

C	T	W	K	J	O	D	J	R	L	B	U	O	D	E	C
P	R	L	D	O	U	B	L	E	L	B	U	O	D	R	R
D	A	O	X	T	W	J	O	I	N	T	E	D	U	D	O
T	Y	P	S	H	J	U	Y	M	M	A	H	W	T	N	S
I	A	O	D	S	T	A	N	D	A	R	D	P	D	E	S
G	L	U	D	O	U	B	L	E	H	T	H	U	O	T	J
I	P	A	R	K	P	D	E	L	B	U	O	D	W	N	D
D	E	C	K	E	R	W	B	U	O	R	E	K	C	E	D

D	O	U	B	L	E	T	J	R	E	D	A	E	H	R	P
I	D	H	E	L	I	X	O	P	O	E	D	E	J	E	Y
G	U	K	B	D	W	H	I	U	K	P	L	J	U	D	M
I	A	U	O	J	T	D	N	A	H	I	L	D	O	A	M
T	O	P	K	U	P	J	T	W	X	J	H	A	T	E	A
D	U	R	W	T	D	O	E	H	X	P	U	D	Y	H	H
T	A	L	K	O	R	A	D	N	A	T	S	U	O	D	W
P	D	O	D	O	U	B	L	E	R	D	N	E	T	N	E

Find these doubly-delicious words: cross, decker, digit, entendre, header, helix, jointed, park, play, standard, take, talk, whammy

Bonus: **How** many **times** can you find **double**, the word?

Pick One

Circle it, write it, explain your choice. You can only pick one. No cheating! This activity gets you thinking outside the box, and maybe, outside the cell.

1 Which is more **irritating**, sandwiches for lunch every day or the guy who won't shower?

2 Which is more **original**, the story you tell a new guy or the way you make a spread?

3 Who is less **reassuring**, your lawyer or the guy who promised to pay you back next week?

4 Who is more **grateful**, the guy who got an early release or the guy who tells everyone he has no money on his books?

5 Which is more **bothersome**, being touched by another guy as he talks to you or someone slamming dominoes?

6 Who is more **liberated**, the guy who does drugs on the outside or the guy who reads his Bible on the inside?

7 Which is less **vicious**, a punch or being honest with someone?

What is most IMPORTANT to you?

Make a list, here, now, on this page, inside these triangles.

Doing what you like is freedom. Liking what you do is happiness.

– Frank Tyger

How many rectangles can YOU find?

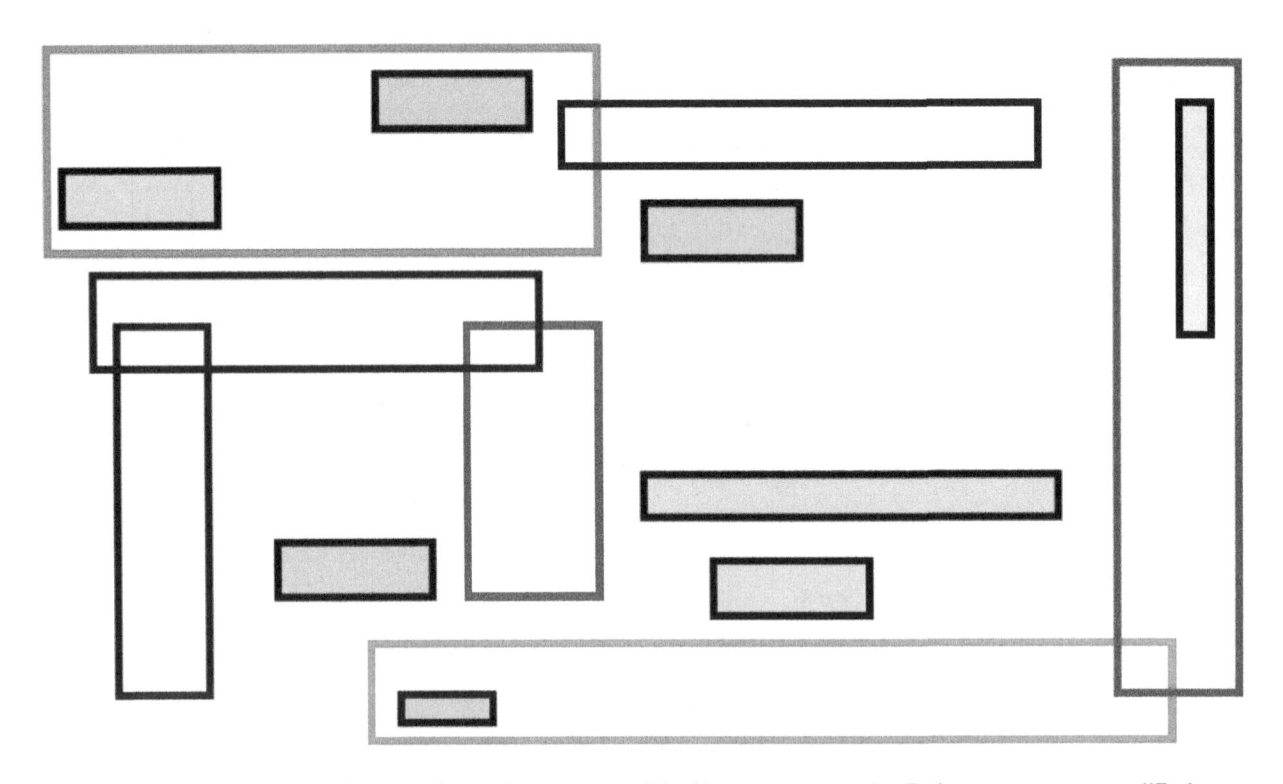

Nothing difficult. Just another puzzle, and me saying "Hi. How are you today? Are you coping well? Are you keeping busy? Are you fighting boredom and winning?" That is your job, by the way, to fill up the long hours that lie in front of you with stuff that makes you happy. If you figure that out, then you'll be fine.

Answers

2	3	5	6	7	9	1	4	8
7	4	9	8	1	5	6	3	2
1	8	6	3	4	2	5	7	9
4	1	3	9	2	7	8	5	6
5	6	8	1	3	4	2	9	7
9	7	2	5	8	6	4	1	3
8	5	4	2	9	3	7	6	1
6	9	1	7	5	8	3	2	4
3	2	7	4	6	1	9	8	5

Scrambled Words: powerful, splinters, divides, birth, strips, shakes

Word Puzzlers: first come...first served, feel it in my bones, everyone, survive

Rectangles: 27

Psalm 29 ends with this: "The LORD will bless His people with peace."

What does this mean to **bless**?

Who are **His people**?

What is **peace**?

Challenge SEVEN

Unscramble these words

> If I am to keep any hold at all of my sanity, I must not _____ on what might have been...to do so would be to go truly _____. It is the one lesson I learned well at the asylum—to _____ each day as it _____, day by day, and to dwell neither on _____ of the past nor _____ about the future—both of which are beyond my _____ to influence.

One Thousand White Women, page 128

moecs   wllde   adm
restrge
oriswre   viel   rowpe

These words came from a novel, a fictionalized version of a real event, from a character who was locked up unfairly, imprisoned in an insane asylum. It's a good book, one you might enjoy if you're interested in what it would have been like for a woman to be traded by the US Government to Indians, as brides, in exchange for peace. She weds a chief and lives a life very unlike her own, enduring not only drastic changes (lack of freedom and choice), but also cruel abuse. How did she survive and go on to live a full and exciting life? Find out. Read it.

Did you know: a ship's **poop deck** is NOT where sailors use the restroom

Word Search

Hey, it's that time again to find words.
No! Not words. Numbers.
123456789.
In order.
From one to nine.
They can be **horizontal**, **vertical**, **diagonal**, **forwards**, or **backwards**.
Good luck!
Now get to work...

1	2	3	4	5	6	7	8	9	8	7	6	5	4	5	1
3	2	4	5	6	7	8	8	9	8	5	4	3	2	3	2
2	3	3	1	2	3	7	7	8	9	4	5	6	7	2	3
1	2	3	4	4	6	5	4	3	2	1	5	3	8	1	4
2	1	2	3	5	6	7	8	8	9	2	9	8	9	8	5
3	5	3	4	1	6	6	7	8	8	3	8	8	2	1	6
1	6	3	9	2	5	7	1	2	7	4	7	9	8	3	7
7	2	1	8	5	4	5	8	9	6	6	6	5	6	9	8
1	3	2	1	2	3	6	7	9	5	1	5	6	7	8	9
4	1	3	4	3	2	3	3	4	4	2	4	4	1	3	3
7	5	4	8	9	1	4	3	7	3	3	3	2	3	1	4
6	1	5	2	1	5	2	5	6	2	4	2	2	5	2	5
5	9	6	5	6	1	3	4	5	1	5	1	1	4	2	1
4	1	7	7	6	3	4	1	4	7	6	5	4	3	2	1
3	9	8	1	8	9	3	4	3	4	7	6	3	4	9	2
2	9	8	7	6	5	4	3	2	1	8	9	1	5	8	3
1	2	3	4	5	4	3	2	1	2	9	8	7	6	5	4

When the **wicked** came against me to EAT up my **FLESH**, my enemies and **foes**, they **stumbled** and **fell**.

Psalm 27:2

3	9	1	8	4	6	7	2	5
5	7	8	3	1	2	9	4	6
6	2	4	5	9	7	3	1	8
1	5	6	4	8	3	2	7	9
8	4	7	1	2	9	6	5	3
2	3	9	6	7	5	1	8	4
9	1	5	2	6	4	8	3	7
7	8	3	9	5	1	4	6	2
4	6	2	7	3	8	5	9	1

Sudoku

1-2-3-4-5-6-7-8-9

A number game, for you.

Enjoy yourself.

Everyone speaks well of the bridge that carries them over.

What does this mean?

1 *"speaks well"* means: _____

2 *"bridge"* means: _____

3 *"carries"* means: _____

4 *"over"* means: _____

The mind is its own place, and in itself can make a heaven of hell, a hell of heaven.

- John Milton

How many rectangles can YOU find?

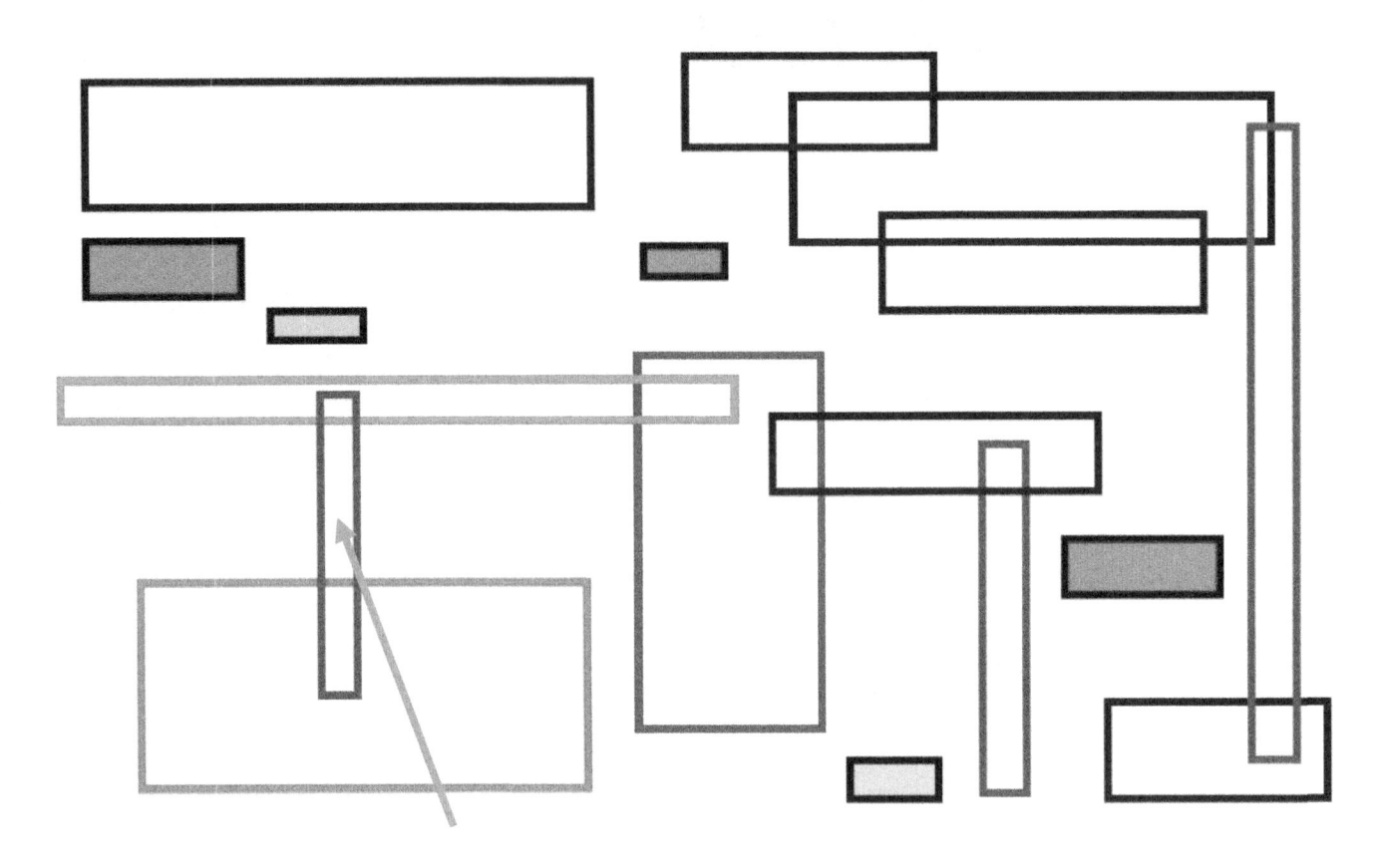

There is a rectangle here that has six rectangles in it. That's right. Six. That vertical, skinny rectangle has three single rectangles, two double rectangles, and one triple rectangle. Now, look elsewhere on this page to find others of similar description.

WORD Puzzlers

Well, here are four more challenges. I shouldn't have to give you any clues by now, because you should be pretty good at figuring these out. Where is the word located? Listen to how something sounds. What is special about what you see? Good luck!

1111111111111 1111111111111 1111111111111 1111111111111 1111111111111 1111111111111 11111111111110	hat
B-10	"Blahblahblahblahblah blahblahblahblahblah blahblahblahblahblah blahblahblahblahblah blahblahblahfamous."

What four words do you see?

(common words or phrases we say)

1. _____
2. _____
3. _____
4. _____

Pick One

Circle it, write it, explain your choice. You can only pick one. No cheating! This activity gets you thinking outside the box, and maybe, outside the cell.

1 Which is more **judgmental**, saying "I told you so" or keeping your thoughts to yourself?

2 Who is less **anxious**, the guy who talks non-stop on the bus ride to court or the guy who sits in silence on his bunk?

3 Which is more **quenching**, a glass of cold water or a dive into an ocean wave?

4 Which is more **boring**, the talker at the Bible study table or that same movie again?

5 Who is more **humble**, the guy who talks about how he feels or the guy who listens?

6 Who is more **trustworthy**, the guy who laughs at your jokes or the guy who keeps to himself?

7 Who is more **unconcerned**, the guy with the blank look in his eyes or the deputy who just walked by?

Tiny filaments show the sun's work, light and warmth that we take for granted. We awake each day and wander outside to do our daily duties, our job, work, and we drive around, music playing while the wind blows past us and the sun shines through our windshield, and we expect it. It just happens. And then one day we find ourselves locked among cold cinderblocks and clanging steel, and that brightness is gone. Ah, the things we take for granted, and miss, free stuff that makes life what it is.

What would you say to heaven's judge IF you were there now?

_____
_____
_____
_____
_____
_____
_____
_____
_____
_____
_____
_____
_____
_____
_____
_____
_____
_____
_____

Answers

3	9	1	8	4	6	7	2	5
5	7	8	3	1	2	9	4	6
6	2	4	5	9	7	3	1	8
1	5	6	4	8	3	2	7	9
8	4	7	1	2	9	6	5	3
2	3	9	6	7	5	1	8	4
9	1	5	2	6	4	8	3	7
7	8	3	9	5	1	4	6	2
4	6	2	7	3	8	5	9	1

Scrambled Words: dwell, mad, live, comes, regrets, worries, power

Word Puzzlers: not the last one, top hat, beaten, famous last words

Rectangles: 31

Every man CASTS a shadow.

Oh really? A shadow? Do I? and you? Of course. But this phrase has little to do with the sun and light and the darkness that is on the other side of me as I walk. It has everything to do with...wait. You tell me. What does this really mean?

_____

_____

_____

_____

Challenge EIGHT

Unscramble these words ↓

The race is not to the _____,
nor the battle to the _____,
nor the bread to the _____,
nor riches to men of _____,
nor favor to men of _____,
But _____ and _____ happen to them all.

Ecclesiastes 9:11

item swift siwe
nreusandtding
ehncac lkisl nosrtg

Think about the words above and what they mean.

What four things happens to everyone

1 We all _____

2 We all _____

3 We all _____

4 We all _____

Word Search

Hey, it's that time again to find words.
They can be **horizontal, vertical, diagonal, forwards,** or **backwards**.
What do these words have in common?
Clue #1: all of them start with the same four letters.
Clue #2: look for those four letters in this puzzle, repeated many times.
Clue #3: back words.

B	A	C	K	B	S	T	O	P	U	B	B	K	S	B	A
O	O	B	B	B	T	B	B	P	B	B	C	T	A	C	B
N	B	A	C	K	A	K	A	A	A	A	O	C	H	B	B
E	B	A	R	B	I	C	C	C	B	R	K	E	T	I	B
S	B	A	C	D	R	A	K	K	Y	B	A	C	K	B	B
B	L	B	C	K	S	B	B	L	B	B	K	C	A	R	T
K	B	I	B	K	H	S	A	W	O	R	D	E	R	B	B
T	C	B	D	B	B	S	B	B	B	K	G	B	B	R	A	F
B	U	A	P	E	H	W	B	S	C	B	A	B	C	I	B
B	B	O	B	B	B	B	A	T	A	B	C	K	E	K	F
B	R	E	S	T	A	L	B	R	B	B	K	L	B	C	D
D	B	B	E	B	C	A	A	E	D	N	D	B	K	A	N
G	B	B	A	C	K	D	C	T	G	S	O	C	B	B	A
B	N	B	P	C	A	E	K	C	K	A	A	M	E	O	H
S	P	I	N	B	K	P	B	H	C	B	T	B	M	B	B
B	L	S	D	O	O	W	S	B	A	B	B	S	B	A	B
F	B	K	L	A	T	B	B	B	B	D	N	U	O	R	G

Find these words: ache, bite, board, bone, drop, field, fire, flip, gammon, ground, hand, hoe, ing, lash, log, order, out, pack, pedal, rest, side, slap, slide, space, spin, stage, stairs, stop, story, stretch, talk, truck, up, wards, wash, woods

Word Puzzlers

Ahhhh!
More of that secret stuff.
For you, and your friends,
or if you'd prefer, those
guys you're stuck living with.
Look carefully at the
direction of the word, or its
location in the box.
And enjoy the challenge.

pre10ding	↓ HELPING HELPING
steFRANKin	DIPPER

What four words do you see?

(common words or phrases we say)

1. _____
2. _____
3. _____
4. _____

An ant crawls across a petal, coming or going, looking for nectar, and I notice it on its way. Does it notice me, the guy standing so close, camera in hand? No. It does not. I'm not important. It doesn't need me or want me in its life. I am a temporary visitor to its world, just like you are in the world you find yourself, behind bars. You are a visitor, one of many, insignificant, irrelevant, just passing through. Don't forget that and overstate your own personal importance. You're just a number and a shadow.

Sudoku

9	6	1	8	3	2	5	4	7
3	2	5	7	1	4	8	6	9
7	8	4	6	5	9	3	1	2
2	9	6	5	4	8	1	7	3
8	1	7	9	2	3	6	5	4
4	5	3	1	7	6	9	2	8
6	7	2	3	9	5	4	8	1
1	3	8	4	6	7	2	9	5
5	4	9	2	8	1	7	3	6

1-2-3-4-5-6-7-8-9

By this point, surely you know what to do with these numbers, just like you know what to do with the truckload of minutes you're stuck with, so many, from breakfast til lights out.

Tell me a little about **numbers** (a few are done for you)

one = _____
two = _____
three = wheels on a tricycle
four = _____
five = _____
six = legs on an ant
seven = days in a week
eight = _____
nine = _____

It is not the strongest that survive, nor the most intelligent, but the one most responsive to change.

— Charles Darwin

How many rectangles can YOU find?

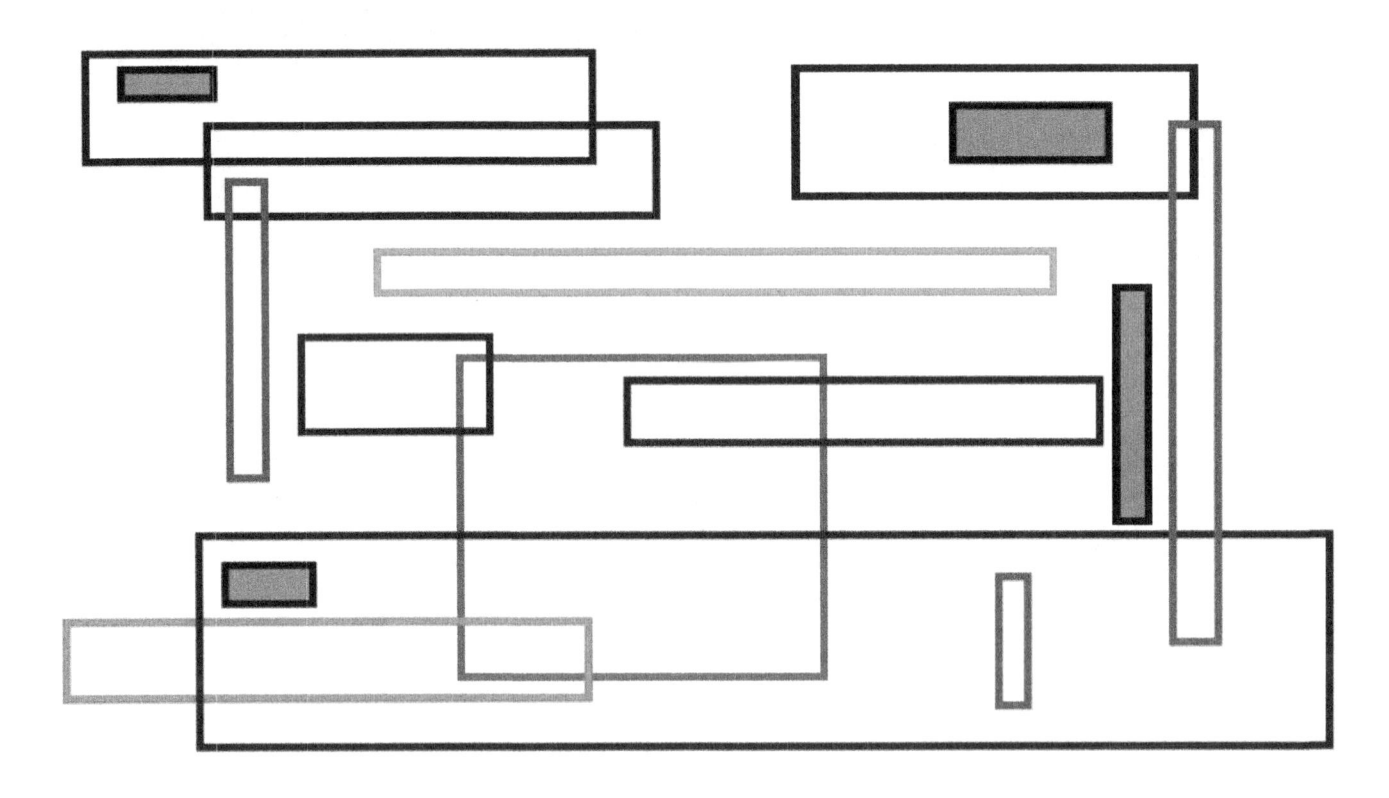

I hope that you've learned from my previous hints. I shouldn't have to give you any more help if you've been paying attention and doing detailed work. If. It's all up to you...

Pick One

Circle it, write it, explain your choice. You can only pick one. No cheating! This activity gets you thinking outside the box, and maybe, outside the cell.

1. Who is more **motivated**, the guy who has a week to go or the prosecutor who just got your case?

2. Who is more **thankful**, the guy who asks for everyone's leftover food or the guy who got two letters today?

3. Which is more **lonely**, the guy who gets no visitors or the guy who is into everyone's business?

4. Who is more **gullible**, the guy who tells everyone that he is innocent or the guys who believe what he says?

5. Who is more **organized**, the guy whose bed is immaculate or the guy who is picking a jury today?

6. Who is more **narrow-minded**, the guy who won't listen or the guy who insults other faiths?

7. Who is more **isolated**, the guy in solitary or the guy who just got jumped for stealing?

Reasons that my life is worth living...
write a few in the spaces below

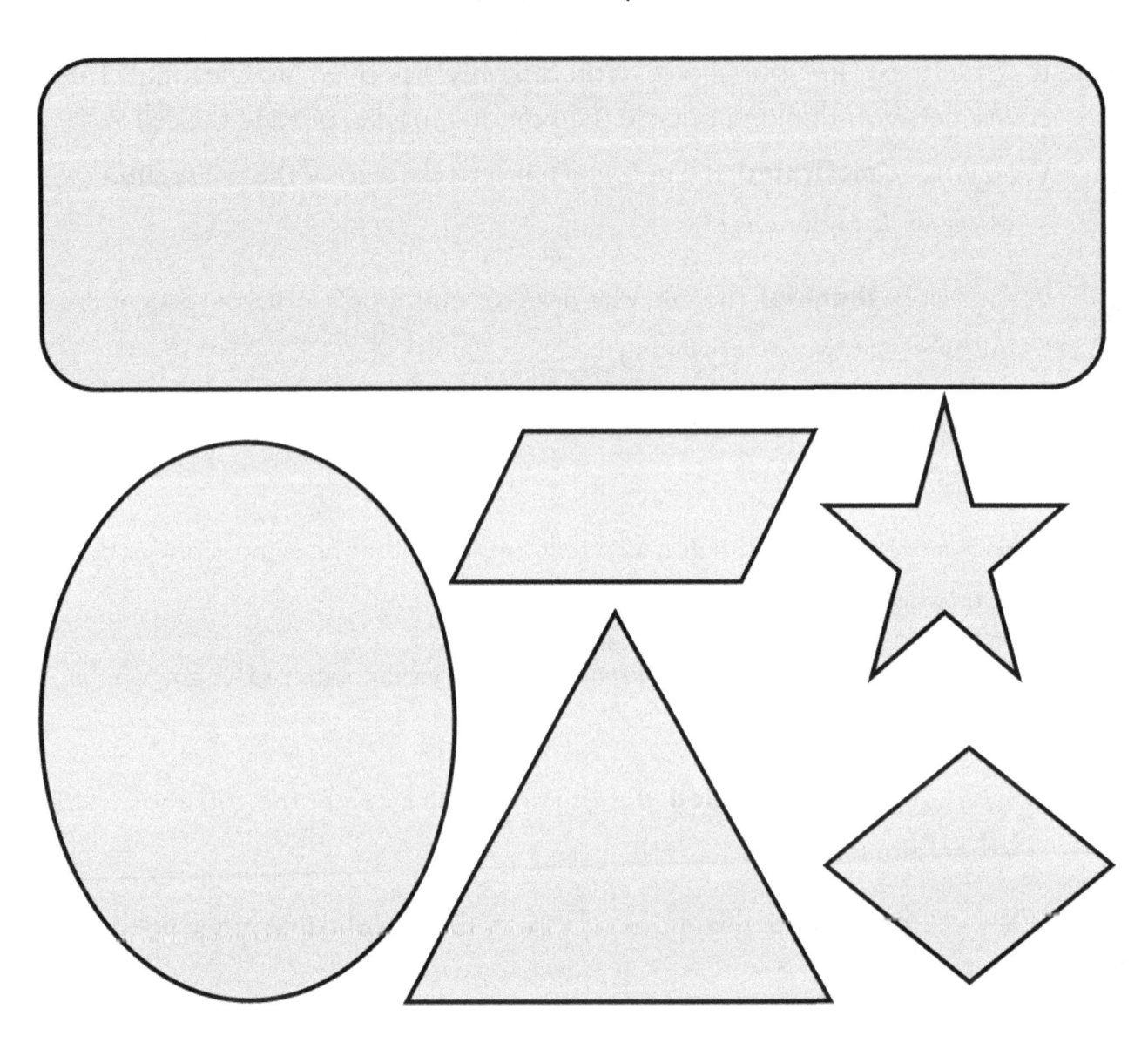

Answers

9	6	1	8	3	2	5	4	7
3	2	5	7	1	4	8	6	9
7	8	4	6	5	9	3	1	2
2	9	6	5	4	8	1	7	3
8	1	7	9	2	3	6	5	4
4	5	3	1	7	6	9	2	8
6	7	2	3	9	5	4	8	1
1	3	8	4	6	7	2	9	5
5	4	9	2	8	1	7	3	6

Scrambled Words: swift, strong, wise, understanding, skill, time, chance

Word Puzzlers: pretending, second helping, Frankenstein, Little Dipper

Rectangles: 29

Don't let YOUR wants overtake YOUR needs.

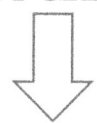

⬇

I know, I know. You want to punch that guy in the face, but you need to stay out of trouble, but you want to show him that you're a man, but you need to get out and take care of your kids, but you want to punch him so bad. Well, which is more important, what you want or what you need? You decide. It's your life.

Challenge NINE

Better a handful with _____ than both hands _____, together with toil and grasping for the _____.

Ecclesiastes 4:6

Unscramble these words

diwn   lufl
tuenqiess

What does that mean?

_____
_____
_____
_____
_____
_____

Did you know: the word **burrito** literally means "little donkey" in Spanish

Time

Time? What do you know about it?

Time never stops, but keeps going, even when we want it to stop just for a moment so we can enjoy it just a little bit longer.

Time has no do-overs. We can't go back in time and change things. We're stuck with the regrets of mistakes, errors, our own selfish acts, forever.

Time is free and costs us nothing. We arrived here without any payment. What we do with it is our choice.

Did you know: the **Heimlich maneuver**, a maneuver to save someone who is choking, was named after an American surgeon, Henry J. Heimlich

That way. It is there, always there, but you aren't at the final gate yet. You have things to do, time to pass, meals to eat, days to do and say and be. One day you'll be at that exit, walking out, but not today. So focus on today, doing what you can to bring a smile to your face and to others. Focus on learning what you can, improving, getting better. Work out. Get good at something like drawing, writing, or telling stories. Read, learn new things, find out and examine. And one day when you leave this place, you'll walk away as a better man, a stronger man, a smarter man.

Sudoku

7	5	6	1	4	2	8	9	3
3	1	2	6	8	9	7	4	5
9	8	4	5	7	3	2	6	1
2	9	8	4	6	1	3	5	7
4	6	1	3	5	7	9	8	2
5	7	3	2	9	8	6	1	4
8	4	9	7	2	5	1	3	6
1	2	5	9	3	6	4	7	8
6	3	7	8	1	4	5	2	9

There are four missing from the first column, and four from the second, and four from the third...

Lots of missing numbers.

Enjoy!

Why are numbers important?

1 We use numbers to _____
2 We use numbers to _____
3 We use numbers to _____
4 We use numbers to _____

Word Search

"Hey, the **evidence** is not good." What a horrible thing to hear from the guy in the suit who gets to go home tonight. Well, hidden in this puzzle is **every** word you might want to find on the **eve** before your hoped-for release. They can be horizontal, vertical, diagonal, forwards, or backwards.

E	V	E	R	V	L	A	C	I	L	E	G	N	A	V	E
E	V	I	V	T	Y	R	E	V	E	V	V	R	E	E	V
E	E	A	E	N	E	E	R	G	R	E	V	E	C	V	E
V	V	E	P	V	Y	R	E	V	E	N	E	V	N	E	N
E	E	E	V	O	K	E	V	E	V	T	V	E	E	R	I
R	R	R	R	E	R	L	I	V	E	U	O	R	D	Y	N
Y	R	E	V	E	R	A	E	R	R	A	L	Y	I	Y	G
E	E	V	E	R	Y	V	T	R	Y	L	U	E	V	R	T
V	R	N	O	I	S	A	V	E	B	L	T	V	E	E	N
E	O	E	E	V	E	R	Y	V	O	Y	I	N	V	V	E
N	M	V	R	E	V	E	R	Y	D	V	O	R	E	E	C
O	R	E	E	V	E	V	E	R	Y	E	N	E	R	V	S
Y	E	R	V	E	V	E	V	V	E	R	V	R	Y	E	E
R	V	Y	D	R	E	V	E	R	Y	R	E	V	E	R	N
E	E	A	E	V	E	R	Y	E	Y	R	E	V	E	Y	A
V	V	E	G	N	I	T	S	A	L	R	E	V	E	E	V
E	V	A	C	U	A	T	E	E	T	A	U	L	A	V	E

Find these words: evacuate, evade, evaluate, evanescent, evangelical, evaporate, evasion, eve, even, evening, event, eventually, ever, evergreen, everlasting, evermore, every, everybody, everyone, evict, evidence, evil, evoke, evolution

Bonus: HOW MANY times can you find **EVEry** word?

How many rectangles can YOU find?

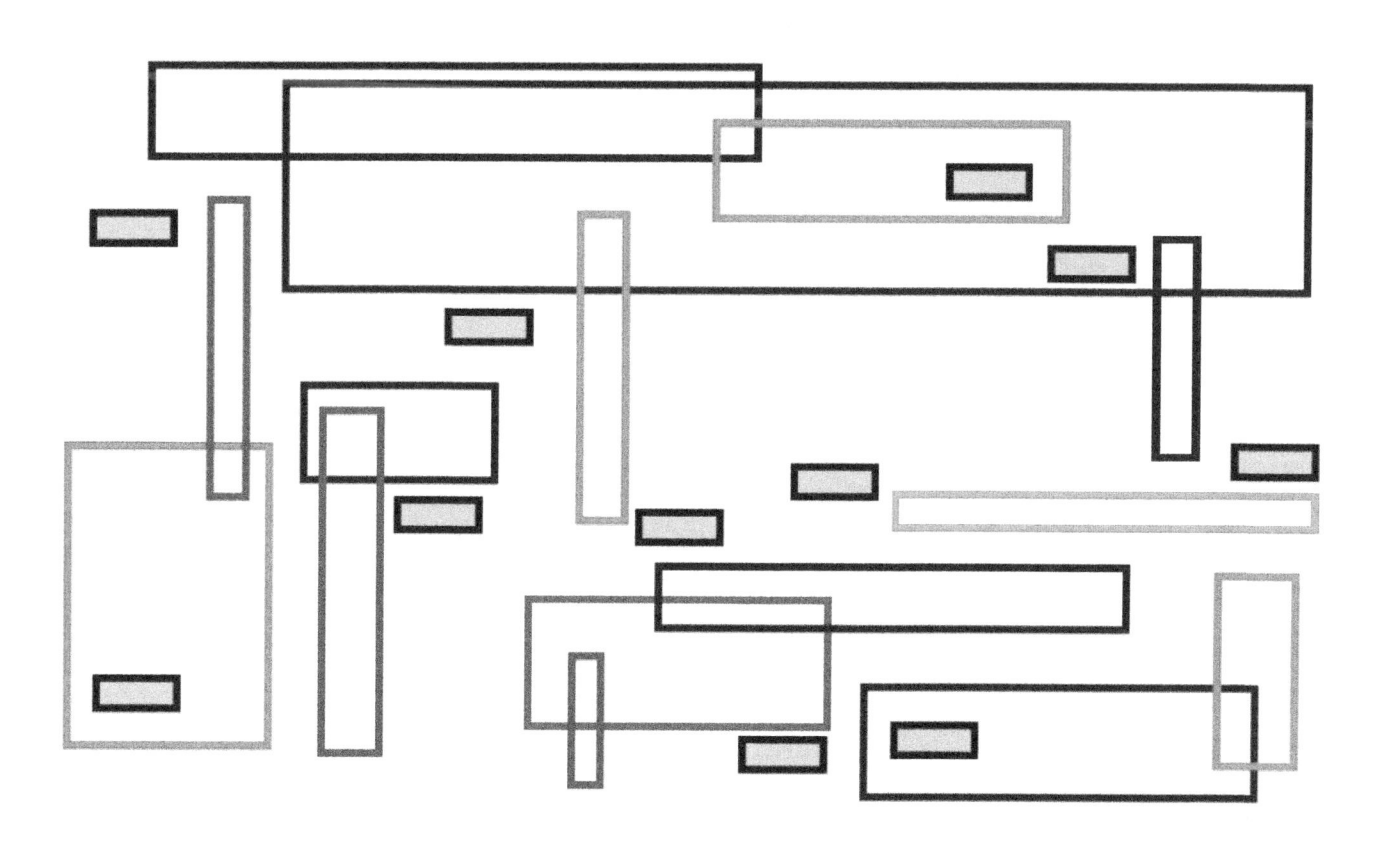

One, two, three...lots. How many did you find?

The problem is not that there are problems. The problem is expecting otherwise and thinking that having problems is a problem.

— Theodore Rubin

Here **is a** *blank* **page,** for **no** reason....

Live this in moment!

Answers

7	5	6	1	4	2	8	9	3
3	1	2	6	8	9	7	4	5
9	8	4	5	7	3	2	6	1
2	9	8	4	6	1	3	5	7
4	6	1	3	5	7	9	8	2
5	7	3	2	9	8	6	1	4
8	4	9	7	2	5	1	3	6
1	2	5	9	3	6	4	7	8
6	3	7	8	1	4	5	2	9

Scrambled Words: quietness, full, wind

Rectangles: 39

Cognitive biases: Predictable patterns of thought and behavior that lead us to drawing incorrect conclusions:

We tend to **look for** information that **confirms** our beliefs.

We tend to **ignore** information that **challenges** our beliefs.

How about you? Yes, you. You do this, as do I and every other biped on this planet. We make a snap judgment and then spend the rest of our time filling in the reasons and proofs. When a new guy walks in, all tatted and angry, do you make a quick judgment? Of course you do. Stop that! It's wrong. Give the guy a chance.

Challenge TEN

Unscramble these words ⬇

My _____ is severely pained within me,

and the _____ of death have fallen upon me.

_____ and _____ have come upon me,

and _____ has overwhelmed me.

So I said, "Oh, that I had _____ like a dove!

I would _____ away and be at _____.

   Indeed, I would wander far off,

   And remain in the wilderness.

treha ster gnwis
nareffuless rrrooh
  ifyr
mertgbiln errrsot

Psalm 55:4-7

Rest. To you, what is rest, the real kind where you feel refreshed afterwards? _____

_____
_____
_____
_____
_____

Missing Letters

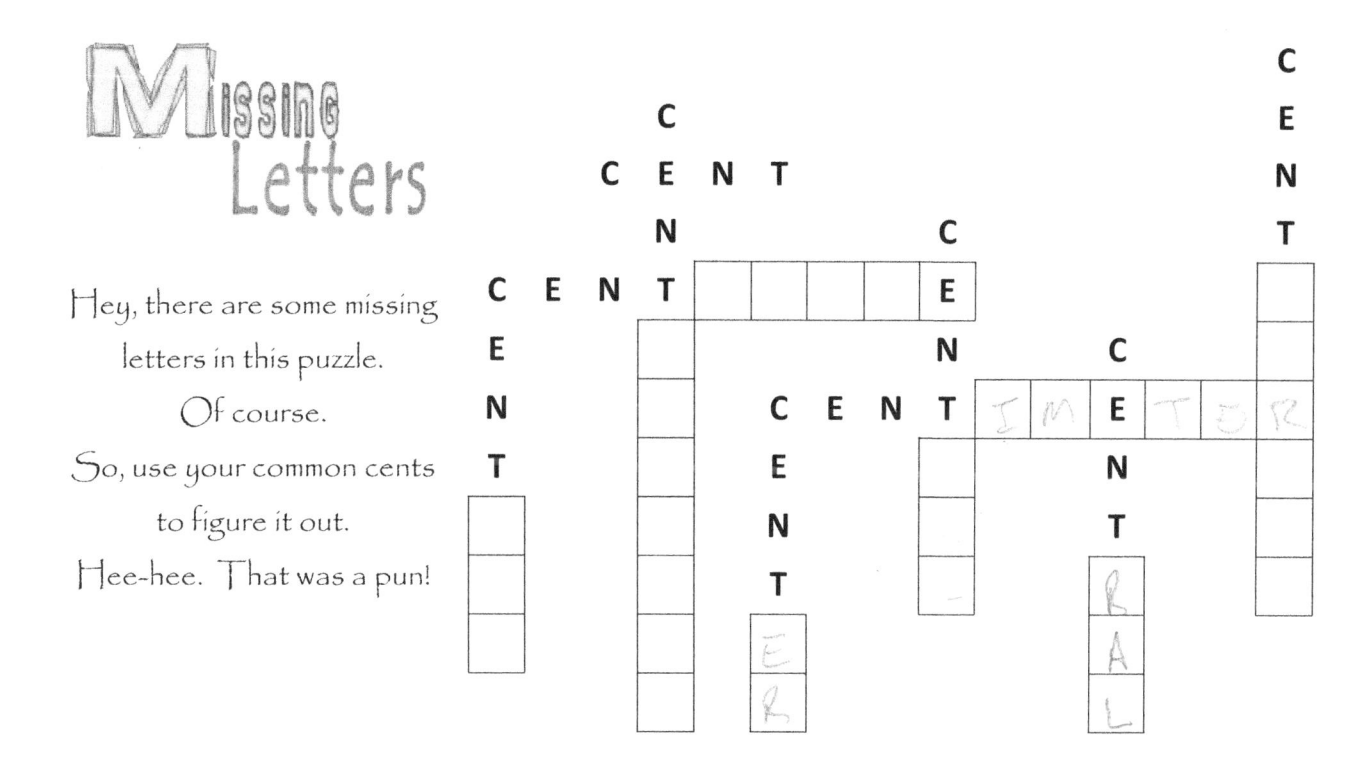

Hey, there are some missing letters in this puzzle. Of course. So, use your common cents to figure it out. Hee-hee. That was a pun!

Use these missing letters to fill in the blanks:

A A A A D D E E E E F G G I I I I L L M P R R R R R R T U U Y

Okay, if you really **NEED** some **clues** because you find this challenge **too much** for your NOGGIN, then here are a few in **cryptic** form: horse-sense, it's so hot, merry-go-round, ten times ten, not left or right, leggy, pinky width, essential.

Sudoku

3	6	9	1	4	8	5	7	2
2	1	7	3	5	6	4	8	9
8	5	4	2	7	9	1	3	6
9	8	3	5	2	1	6	4	7
5	2	6	4	9	7	8	1	3
4	7	1	8	6	3	2	9	5
7	4	8	6	3	5	9	2	1
6	9	2	7	1	4	3	5	8
1	3	5	9	8	2	7	6	4

It's that time again.

1-2-3-4-5-6-7-8-9

TEN.

Why did I just put "ten" there?

Rhyme time?

Stand on your own two **feet**.

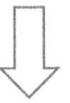

⇩

Wise sayings often means more than just what you see. This little bit of advice is NOT really talking about your actual feet. What is it talking about?

stand =

feet =

The same moon that your loved ones see is the one you see. Look up there, imagine what they're doing, how they're feeling, what is in their lives today. And then get busy doing something yourself. Time isn't replaceable. You don't become better by sleeping all day, or playing cards or dominoes or watching television. Do something with the time you have, because that moon will travel across the sky by day and night, never stopping, going around and around, while you're doing something or not.

How many rectangles can YOU find?

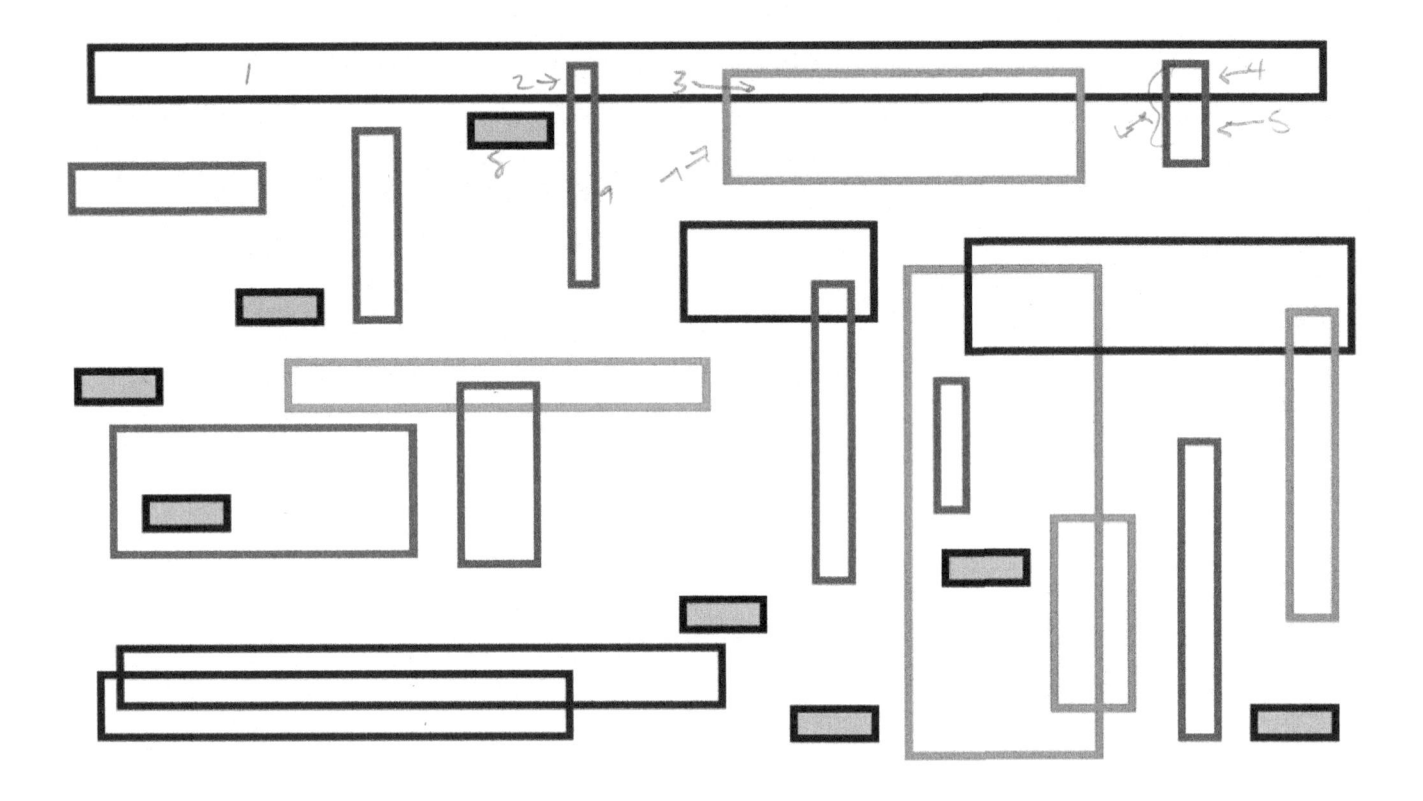

This is it, the final design. Yep, ten of them, all done, all gone, no more for you to work on. Sorry. That's just the way it is. Every beginning has an end, or was it "every ruse has its thorn"?

Word Puzzlers

Ahhhh!
More of that secret stuff. For you, and your friends, or if you'd prefer, those guys you're stuck living with. Look carefully at the direction of the word, or its location in the box. And enjoy the challenge.

| **F8** | ↓ _____READING_____ |
| speed | T T T T T
T |

What four words do you see?

(common words or phrases we say)

1. _____
2. _____
3. _____
4. _____

Pick One

Circle it, write it, explain your choice. You can only pick one. No cheating! This activity gets you thinking outside the box, and maybe, outside the cell.

1	Which is more **pathetic**, the guy who cried at night or the guy who brags about his crime?
2	Which is more **exotic**, a sexy dancer or a life of drugs?
3	Which is more **disruptive**, a crazy guy at night or an angry guy in the day?
4	Who is more **vengeful**, a victim's family or a cop you lied to?
5	Who is more **argumentative**, a guy who takes from others or a guy who injects drugs?
6	Who is more **jealous**, a boyfriend in jail or a guy who never gets to order from the store/commissary?
7	Which is more **worried**, the guy who is on his way to court or the guy who is going to prison for the first time?

The secret of health for both mind and body is not to mourn for the past, worry about the future, or anticipate problems, but to live in the present moment wisely and earnestly.

- Buddha

What would you write here IF you could?
Psst! YOU can!

_____
_____
_____
_____
_____
_____
_____
_____
_____
_____
_____
_____
_____
_____
_____
_____

Answers

3	6	9	1	4	8	5	7	2
2	1	7	3	5	6	4	8	9
8	5	4	2	7	9	1	3	6
9	8	1	5	2	3	6	4	7
5	2	6	4	9	7	8	1	3
4	7	3	8	6	1	2	9	5
7	4	8	6	3	5	9	2	1
6	9	2	7	1	4	3	5	8
1	3	5	9	8	2	7	6	4

Scrambled Words: heart, terrors, fearfulness, trembling, horror, wings, fly, rest

Missing Letters: centrifugal, centaur, centipede, center, central, century, centimeter, centigrade

Rectangles: 42

Word Puzzlers: fate, reading between the lines, hi-speed, sixty

"I **wish** I had the **courage** to live a life **true** to myself, not the life **OTHERS** expect of me."

-someone with regrets

Your thoughts: _____

_____

_____

_____

_____

ONE of my Books
you might want to check out...

Improve yourself
while in jail or prison

ANOTHER of my Books you might want to check out...

Anger Management
Jail/Prison Bible Study Series, vol. 1

A wise man controls his TEMPER. He knows that ANGER causes mistakes.

What are your PLANS for when you finish serving your sentence in jail/prison, and you are free to go where you want?

Where is your SAFE PLACE to calm down and get back in control of your emotions after you are angered?

Describe two moments today when you were calm inside even though there was annoying noise or chaos all around you.

Is there a difference between what you FEEL on the inside and what you DO on the outside?

Tell about a moment in jail/prison that involved someone's anger directed at you.

Always be willing to LISTEN and slow to speak

ANOTHER of my Books
you might want to check out...

Surviving the Stress
A Gift for a Loved One in Jail or Prison

Other Jail/Prison books you might be interested in:

> If someone in your family is ordering this for you, remind them to purchase a new copy from Amazon (most county jails and state prisons will not accept books from an outside vendor). All my books are available through Amazon, just search for "C. Mahoney" and the title. Or, search for "Mahoney jail or prison".

Keeping the Mind Active in Jail or Prison - Hidden Secrets
Keeping the Mind Active in Jail or Prison - Optical Illusions
Keeping the Mind Active in Jail or Prison - Visual Puzzles

Anger Management (**Jail/Prison Bible Study Series**, Vol 1)
Finding Happiness (**Jail/Prison Bible Study Series**, Vol 2)
Learning to Listen (**Jail/Prison Bible Study Series**, Vol 3)
Patiently Waiting (**Jail/Prison Bible Study Series**, Vol 4)
Peaceful Respect (**Jail/Prison Bible Study Series**, Vol 5)
Kindness to Others (**Jail/Prison Bible Study Series**, Vol 6)

Surviving the Stress: a gift for a loved one in jail or prison
Surviving the Insanity: a gift for a loved one in jail or prison
Doing More Than Survive: a gift for a loved one in jail or prison

75 Fun Facts to Help you Beat the Boredom of Jail or Prison
75 Interesting Facts to Help you Beat the Boredom of Jail or Prison
75 Strange Facts to Help you Beat the Boredom of Jail or Prison
75 Weird Facts to Help you Beat the Boredom of Jail or Prison
250 Things to Write about...in jail
Become a Better Writer in Jail or Prison
Encouraging Words for someone in Jail or Prison
Improve yourself while in Jail or prison
Making Choices - A book of Moral Dilemmas for Someone in Jail or Prison

Psalm 119 - A Study Guide for Someone in Jail or Prison
Questions for Someone in Jail or Prison
Sudoku for the Guy in Jail or Prison
Surviving Jail or Prison - Creative Writing to Help You Grow
Surviving Jail or Prison - Making Better Choices
Surviving Jail or Prison - Questions to Think About
Surviving Jail or Prison - Thinking About my Life
Thinking and Writing while in Jail or Prison - Exploring African Wisdom
Thinking and Writing while in Jail or Prison - Exploring Buddhist Wisdom
Thinking and Writing while in Jail or Prison - Exploring Native American Wisdom
Thinking and Writing while in Jail or Prison - Exploring The Wisdom of Confucius
Thinking and Writing while in Jail or Prison - Exploring the Wisdom of Gandhi
Thinking and Writing while in Jail or Prison - Exploring Unitarian Universalist Wisdom
Thinking and Writing while in Jail or Prison - Exploring Zoroastrian Wisdom
Word Puzzles to keep the mind sharp in Jail

<u>Wildlife Bible</u> (This is a very cool collection 250 Bible verses and 250 wildlife photos that I took…250 pages that you won't find anywhere else.)